THE
CONSERVATIVE
PARTY

THE CONSERVATIVE PARTY

The First 150 Years

Sheila Moore

Foreword by the Rt Hon. Margaret Thatcher MP

Kevin

Merry Christmas   1982

Frances.

Country Life Books

Published by Country Life Books
Holman House, 95 Sheen Road, Richmond upon Thames, Surrey, TW9 1YJ
and distributed for them by
The Hamlyn Publishing Group Limited
London . New York . Sydney . Toronto
Astronaut House, Feltham, Middlesex, England

First published 1980

ISBN 0 600 36777 0

Set in 11 on 13 Linotron Bembo by
Tradespools Limited, Frome, Somerset

Printed and bound in Great Britain by
Fakenham Press Limited, Fakenham, Norfolk

Contents

Foreword
by Rt Hon. Margaret Thatcher MP

The story of the Conservative party is a marvellous tale, full of all the colour and drama and passion that have marked the history of the British people. It is often forgotten today that politics are not about economic statistics; they are about people and how they want to live, and what sort of society they want to live in.

The Conservative party in particular is about people – as this book so vividly demonstrates – a great chain of people stretching back into the past and forward into the future – a 'partnership', as Edmund Burke said, 'between those who are living, those who are dead, and those who are yet to be born'. These people have been – are –and will be – of all kinds and conditions; their rich variety and enormous diversity is their most appealing characteristic, but they are all linked by their belief in human freedom, in Britain's greatness, and in their own power and responsibility to contribute to both.

Conservatives do not believe – and I do not – that history is writ clear and unchallengeable, or is predestined by economic or any other 'laws'. History is made by people: its movement depends on small currents as well as great tides, on the ideas, the perceptions and the will of all the people of the nation. There have been great leaders in the Conservative party – Peel, showing how to change but not destroy; Disraeli with his call for us to become one nation, not two; Churchill with his matchless courage leading the country through its darkest hours. There have been great leaders, but equally important have been the hundreds of thousands who have worked, and the millions and millions who have voted for the Conservative party and all it stands for.

Something else this book reminds us of, that is too often forgotten in the fury of contemporary elections, is that politics also can be fun, and that through the work and in the activities of the party people have often found their firmest friends. Along with earnest speeches and endless envelopes there have also been, through all these years, wining and dining and dancing and singing, and good conversation and much laughter.

I feel at once both humble and very proud to be the leader of this great party, whose history is so much part of the history of Britain. And it is on a knowledge of this history that I, and I believe most Conservatives, base our optimism for the future. Our past is proof of the courage, honesty and flair of the British people, of their ability to change and to create, and I am confident that our future will be shaped again by these qualities, which have so enriched our past.

Margaret Thatcher

Introduction

by Lord Blake, Provost of Queen's College, Oxford

IN 1880 the Conservative party suffered what seemed a major set-back. After nearly 30 years of opposition interspersed by brief minority governments, they had in 1874 won a major victory under Disraeli, only to see six years later the triumphant return of Gladstone with a majority of over a hundred.

'The situation,' Disraeli wrote to Lord Lytton, 'requires youth and energy. When they are found – and they will be found – I shall make my bow. In the meantime I must act as if I were still young and vigorous and take all steps in my power to sustain the spirit and restore the discipline of the Tory party. They have existed for more than a century and a half as an organised political connection and having survived the loss of the American colonies, the first Napoleon and Lord Grey's Reform Act they must not be snuffed out.'

They were indeed far from being snuffed out, however dismal the scene must then have seemed. One of the fascinating features of the history of political parties is its endless vicissitudes. Sometimes we have the triumph of yesterday succeeded by the disaster of today and the recovery of tomorrow; but there is no regular pattern, and at other times a party may have a long run of unbroken success or failure.

Few people would have predicted in 1880 that, after losing yet another election five years later, the Conservatives would from 1886 have a period of almost unbroken ascendancy for over nineteen years, interrupted only by the weak and fleeting interlude of the Gladstone–Rosebery government of 1892–95. Nor would many people have guessed after the 'Khaki election' of 1900 that only six years later the Conservatives were to sustain the worst defeat in the whole of their history before or since, that it would require a world war to bring them back – and then only as a section of a coalition. There are other examples of this unpredictability. To take one nearer our own time, it would have been a bold prophet who would have guessed that Winston Churchill's narrow win of 1951 (based actually on a minority of votes cast) was to be the precursor of thirteen years of Conservative rule during which the party won two more electoral victories with increased numbers on each occasion.

There can be much argument about when the Conservative party began, and Sheila Moore sketches some of the problems. The name 'Conservative' was first used in an article in the *Quarterly Review* in 1830, but there is a clear connection with the older word 'Tory' which is still often used. Both 'Whig' and 'Tory' originated in the disputes over the Exclusion Act in the crisis of 1679, and were terms of abuse subsequently adopted as defiant symbols of self-esteem (like the 'Old Contemptibles' of the First World War). A 'Whig' was a Scottish horse thief. The name was first applied to Presbyterian rebels and extended to the supporters of Ashley's attempt to keep the future James II from the throne. A 'Tory' was originally an Irish papist outlaw, and the name was later applied to the supporters of Charles II's legitimate heir. As long as the succession to the throne remained a political issue – and it did so till 1745 – the words had some meaning. But the Whigs had become by then, if not before, such an overwhelming majority that Britain was virtually a one-party state. It is not till the great battle between Pitt and Fox in the crisis of 1782–84 that we can see a new division of parties. Pitt (the younger) never called himself a Tory, but Canning, his self-appointed spiritual successor, did, and one can trace a line of political descent from then onwards to Peel and 'Conservatism'.

The party of Pitt, whatever its correct name in an era when 'party' was far less omnipresent than today, effectively ruled, with a brief gap, from his death in 1806 to 1830. It suited Disraeli whose sense of past history was closely entwined with his sense of current politics – especially his own personal role – to treat this as a dismal period of second rate reactionaries. He stigmatised Lord Liverpool (Prime Minister 1812–27) as 'the Arch Mediocrity'. History, as far as English politics are concerned, tended for long years to be written by either liberal academics or romantic Tory radicals. Neither had much good to say of the Liverpool regime, and Shelley and Byron were on their side – the two most brilliant, articulate and prejudiced poets of their day. But Liverpool and his colleagues were trying to achieve something quite important – law and order in a turbulent revolutionary era in a country faced with formidable foreign threats. It is not for Conservatives in the last twenty years of the 20th century to disregard entirely the lessons of those years. The party need not be ashamed to trace its lineage back rather further than Peel.

Yet Peel is indubitably the first great 'Conservative' Prime Minister to bear the name. With the ever-changing problems of the contemporary world there are ever-different lessons to be drawn from the past or, perhaps one should say, ever-different pieces of the past from which to draw lessons. Peel has always had a somewhat uncertain place in the Conservative Pantheon. Like Ramsay MacDonald in 1931 he took a decision in 1846 which broke up his party and left him in the minority (Gladstone who also broke up his party was either luckier or cleverer and kept the majority with him after 1886). But – also like MacDonald – Peel was right. MacDonald saw that Britain would go bankrupt if the party faithful were allowed to have their way. Peel saw that Britain would never achieve prosperity or escape from the dangers of poverty and revolution if the High Tory squires were allowed to preserve the Corn Laws and prevent free trade. He passionately believed that prosperity and freedom went hand in hand. It was Gladstone who said that money should 'fructify in the pockets of the people', but Gladstone thought of himself as a Conservative till 1859 and to his dying day regarded Peel as his master.

A final point about the Liverpool–Peel era (also relevant to a great figure in the Conservative intellectual hierarchy, Edmund Burke, who died earlier) is that it was one of the few periods in the history of the last two centuries when the power of government and the number of government servants was actually reduced. Burke's policy of 'economical reform' followed by successive governments, admittedly not all Tory or Conservative (the Whigs were in from 1830 to 1841), but largely so, saw a real reduction in government expenditure and government employees. The lessons of the past do not always apply to the present. History never exactly repeats itself. But the defeatists who say that the advance of the bureaucracy is irreversible ought at least to look at this period. They may conclude that nothing is irreversible if one is sufficiently anxious to reverse it.

Most Conservatives regard Disraeli as more congenial than Peel and would support him in his great duel against his leader. Disraeli certainly was a much more interesting and intriguing personality, and he was also more modern in his recognition of the role of party. Peel's legacy to the country was prosperity and economic progress; to the Party it was political disaster and a deep determination never to be broken up again. Almost every subsequent leader shared this conviction. One can respect Peel for doing what he did while recognising that the occasions for producing such a traumatic shock ought to be very rare indeed. In fact there has been no comparable parliamentary split in the Conservative party from that day to this.

The public expects the Conservatives to be united, whereas it expects the Labour party, just as it expected the Liberals in the past, to be in a perpetual state of warring faction. Therefore when symptoms, even mild ones, of Conservative division appear, the media (which, after all, usually only reflect what the public is interested in) are particularly observant, and the consequences are liable to be particularly newsworthy – a fact which perhaps should be borne in mind by those whose consciences impel them to give tongue at all often.

Disraeli's external policy as Prime Minister of a great imperial power, however interesting historically, probably has less relevance to us nowadays than other aspects of his astonishing career. Perhaps the most remarkable point which it illustrates is the ability of the Conservatives who might at first sight be regarded as the most traditionalist of the political parties to choose an unorthodox leader if circumstances demanded. Obviously they do not normally do so. Peel, Salisbury, Balfour, Baldwin, Churchill, Eden, Macmillan fit into a traditional pattern. But Disraeli, debt-ridden eccentric adventurer-cum-novelist, Bonar Law, a Canadian-born Presbyterian businessman of Ulster extraction, and Margaret Thatcher, a woman, exemplify the party's ability to look outside the usual circles and seek for talent appropriate to the occasion.

If there is a lesson to be drawn from Sheila Moore's illuminating and entertaining survey it is the almost inexhaustible adaptability and vitality of the Conservative party. Of course it gets fossilised every now and then into archaic and irrelevant attitudes. One such period followed the 'landslide' of 1906 when the party abused the powers of the House of Lords with consequences which have adversely affected the British constitution ever since. Indeed there are many Conservatives who believe that something ought to be done about this as soon as the opportunity arises, if only to forestall abolition by some future – even distantly future – Labour government. If there is one lesson which should be drawn from Disraeli's career it is that there is nothing 'Conservative' about conserving the constitutional settlements of your enemies. The modern Conservative has no more reason to conserve the Parliament Act of 1949 than Derby and Disraeli to conserve the Reform Act of 1832. Harold Macmillan saw this. If he had survived as long in political life as in private life we might have had a rational second chamber by now.

There is another danger which it is difficult for any political party to escape, and it applies to the other side too; this is an adverse change in the atmosphere of that intangible, mysterious but not the less real entity, 'the climate of opinion'. In the third quarter of the 19th century it was hostile to the Conservative party, and no amount of reorganisation of the machine or reshuffling of personalities would have altered the fact. Lord Derby during 22 years lost five general elections in succession, but the party, less febrile than politicians on all sides are today, showed sense in not evicting him; it would have made no difference whatever if they had. In the 1880s the climate changed – no one can really say quite why – and the Liberals were the losers.

Jumping a couple of generations one can see how the climate in the late 1940s altered after the heyday of Attlee in favour of the Conservatives, only to go markedly against them in the early 1960s. A well-known sign of such changes is the tendency of the party in office and under pressure to adopt its opponents' remedies. Harold Wilson claimed the virtues of a 'bonfire of controls' a year or so before Attlee was defeated. The Conservatives became keen on economic planning as they approached the election of 1964. Mr Callaghan after 1976 discovered the virtues of small businesses.

But this book is a history of the past, not a prediction of the future, and those who use the past to predict the future are liable to make mistakes. The lesson of history, it has been said, is that history has no lessons. I do not quite believe this, but it is certain that one's choice of lessons has to be very selective. All that can be said is that the oldest political party in Britain, arguably the oldest in the world, has survived many a defeat only to fight again and win another day. Age has not withered it nor has custom staled its remarkable variety.

R.B.

CHAPTER I
The Leaders

ON PAPER, a Tory leader's power is absolute: selecting the cabinet, determining policy, appointing all the chief party officers. In practice this enormous power is held on loan by the consent of the party in Parliament and the country. If the party loses confidence in the leader, consent is withdrawn, and the leader topples. Or rather – as it is the Conservative party – makes a dignified exit. Of the fifteen Conservative leaders since the beginning of the modern party around 1830, no less than seven have been forced (or 'encouraged') to resign, and all the others (save only Lord Derby) have at some time fought off determined efforts to unseat them.

The most spectacular downfall was Sir Robert Peel's in 1846. Peel had rescued the party from its post-Reform Act shambles in 1832 and brought it to a sweeping victory in 1841. Yet when he repealed the tariff on imported grain (the famous Corn Laws) he so enraged a section of his Parliamentary followers that they voted to bring his government down, cleft the party irretrievably in two, and sent it into the electoral wilderness for nearly 30 years. 'They are blind with fury,' said a member of Peel's cabinet, warning him of the impending vote, 'and seek to wreak their vengeance on you.'

On the other hand, Stanley Baldwin successfully repelled repeated attacks in 1930–31, including one that appeared so invincible *The Times* actually had a leader set up headlined 'Mr Baldwin withdraws'. Baldwin saved himself with a series of masterly speeches, and carried on as leader for another seven years. When Churchill's Chief Whip told him in 1947 that a number of his senior colleagues wanted him to retire, Churchill (according to the Whip) 'reacted violently, banging the floor with his stick'. This proved equally effective, and Churchill carried on for another eight years.

However, the ever-present possibility of withdrawal of the party's consent, underscored by salutary examples of fallen predecessors, means a modern Conservative leader must be constantly aware of, and take account of, the feelings of the followers. When the followers are pleased, the leader has tremendous authority. The minutes of 100 years of party conferences ring with fulsome praise of popular leaders: 'I believe that with Lord Woolton to guide us and with Mr Churchill to lead us we have no fear of the future,' declaimed a conference speaker in 1947.

Other party records reveal what happens when the followers are not pleased: 'I own to being simply appalled by the attitude of the people at the top of our party,' wrote the Conservative editor of the *National Review* in a letter in 1911, 'and above all by their total failure to realise that a continuance of Balfourism means general ruin.' This outburst was just part of an ultimately successful campaign to depose Balfour.

For years, when a new Conservative leader was needed, he was not elected: he 'emerged' in a mysterious process consisting mainly of quiet chats in House of Commons corridors between party Whips and Members whose opinions mattered. 'Great leaders of parties are not elected, they are evolved,' said Capt. the Rt Hon. Ernest Pretyman MP

Sir Robert Peel

1788–1850

Member of Parliament 1809–50
Leader of the party 1830–46
Prime Minister 1834–35,
    1841–46

'WITHOUT PEEL's reforms,'
said the historian Asa Briggs,
'there would have been no golden
age of Victorian Britain.'

Peel sat in Parliament for over
40 years, throughout the violent
times when Britain struggled to
transform from a rural to an
industrial and from an aristocratic
to a democratic nation. Peel
undoubtedly helped ease this
transformation: among other
things he completely revamped
the criminal code, founded the
Metropolitan Police, legalised
trade unions, took women and
children out of the mines, and
limited the brutal length of the
working day. He was proudest,
however, of his financial reforms,
which stabilised the currency and
underpinned the massive Victorian investment in railroads,
industry and empire.

But Peel was a statesman, not a
partisan, and it is one of history's
great ironies that he both created
the modern Conservative party
and nearly destroyed it. Peel built
a powerful, recognisably modern
party from the sulky remnants
left (185 MPs out of 658 in the
1832 Parliament) after the
Catholic Emancipation and
Reform Act battles, and then he
sundered it irrevocably by repealing the Corn Laws in 1846. It was
nearly 30 years before the splin-
tered half under Disraeli regained
power.

Richard Cobden, his political
enemy for a generation, said after
the crash that Peel was 'a Minister
who thought more of the lives of
the people than his own continuance in power'.

Power, however, had never
been Peel's first love. He had an
intensely close, almost insular
marriage, and after the final crisis
when he tumbled from the
heights, he could write, with
every evidence of sincerity: 'Lady
Peel and I are here, quite alone,
feasting on solitude and repose,
and I have every disposition to
forgive my enemies for having
conferred upon me the blessing of
loss of power.'

Edward Stanley

(14th Earl of Derby) 1799–1869

Member of Parliament 1820, went to
    Lords 1844
Leader of the party 1846–68
Prime Minister 1852 (10 months),
    1858–59 (16 months), 1866–68

EDWARD STANLEY, 14th
Earl of Derby, handsome dashing
heir to one of the richest and most
ancient estates of the realm, led
the Conservative party for 22
years, the longest tenure of any
leader, and yet he is now wholly
overshadowed by the giant
figures of his political opponent
Palmerston and his party successor Disraeli.

Derby took over leadership
(reluctantly) of the breakaway
'Protectionists' after the Corn
Law debacle, when the leading
Conservative Ministers remained
unrepentant Peelites. He struggled (unsuccessfully) to reunite
Protectionists and Peelites, and
(ultimately successfully) to
rehabilitate his party's public
image as one competent to
govern.

Derby's period as leader was a
time of loose party discipline and
confused party loyalties (he actually asked Palmerston to join his
1852 minority government). He
was Prime Minister only during
the brief intervals when the Whig
coalitions fell apart, and never had
a parliamentary majority. His
most important contribution historically was to back Disraeli in
giving the vote to working class
householders in 1867, although he
had morosely described it as 'a
leap in the dark'.

sternly in 1921. 'The leader is there and we all know it when he is there.'

However, Members not consulted never found this method very satisfactory, nor did it suit the mood of a more democratic age. So in 1965 a formal election procedure was adopted whereby sitting Conservative MPs choose one of their number as leader by means of a secret ballot. This reform was undoubtedly hastened by an unseemly (and most un-Tory) public struggle for the leadership in 1963. At that time, Prime Minister Harold Macmillan, seriously ill, had his resignation announced actually during the party conference, and thus transformed that normally sedate gathering into a seething political battlefield. Sir Alec Douglas-Home emerged the victor, but the shock to Conservatives of such an unprecedented display of party strife encouraged adoption of the formal process. In theory the leader must now stand for re-election every year, but in practice an actual ballot takes place only following a direct challenge.

For a party whose very name as well as public image implies a conservative approach, the Tories have often been startlingly radical in their choice of leaders: Peel, the son of a provincial millowner, was an industrialist and became Tory leader when the political establishment was wholly dominated by the landed aristocracy.

Disraeli, the avowed creator of the modern Conservative party, was born a Jew at a time when anti-Semitism was rife. Exotic, extravagant, passionate in his denunciation of the Establishment and his defence of the disadvantaged, with bejewelled fingers and ringlets in his hair, Disraeli would appear the least likely person to lead Victorian Conservatives. Yet even today, over 100 years on, he is the one leader most quoted by other Conservative politicians.

Even more unlikely was Bonar Law, a blunt dour-faced Scottish iron merchant who was chosen (albeit by default when the two top contenders withdrew) to lead the urbane sophisticated Edwardian Tories.

Then in 1975 the Conservatives astonished popular opinion again when they elected as their leader Margaret Thatcher, the first woman ever to head a major Western political party.

Above left *Disraeli dominated the House of Commons with his brilliant passionate oratory, and his sharp witty tongue made him the darling of London's powerful political hostesses.*

Above right *The 3rd Marquess of Salisbury, here with two more Cecils, was happiest behind the iron gates at Hatfield, surrounded by his family. But the historian Robert Rhodes James says he was 'the most formidably equipped politician for all seasons since Robert Cecil, 1st Earl of Salisbury, had made his family's eminence and fame'.*

15

Benjamin Disraeli

(1st Earl of Beaconsfield) 1804–81

Member of Parliament 1837, went to
  Lords 1876
Leader of the party 1868–81
Prime Minister 1868 (8 months),
  1874–80

DISRAELI, SAYS Lord Blake, was 'the most extraordinary, incongruous, fascinating, fresh and timeless figure ever to have led the Conservative party'. That he led it at all was a triumph of talent and tenacity over formidable odds. As an impoverished, exotically dressed novelist with a razor-sharp tongue, Disraeli excited deep suspicion in the party: 'I would not trust Disraeli any more than I would a committed felon,' wrote Beresford, the Chief Whip, to Stanley in 1847. But Queen Victoria came to call him her 'dear and valued friend', and upon his death a national movement – the Primrose League – was founded in his honour.

Disraeli's dazzling destructive Parliamentary performances were in large part responsible for the downfall of Peel and the party in 1846, but it was the same oratorical skill that restored the party's self-confidence in the 1850s and 1860s and defined the enduring themes of modern Conservatism – themes that have been invoked by every leader since. 'The Conservative party is a national party,' said Disraeli, and its abiding concerns are 'to maintain the institutions of the country' and 'to elevate the condition of the people'.

In the teeth of anxious opposition from his own colleagues, Disraeli had the political vision not only to extend the franchise without splitting the party, but at the same time to create an effective organisation to harvest the new votes. It was an organisation so prescient and resilient that its basic structure remains unchanged to this day. His second administration, formed when he was nearly 70, passed one of the largest chunks of reformist social legislation of the century.

Like Peel, Disraeli was supported by an unusually successful marriage, although when he wed Mary Ann – frivolous, newly widowed, and twelve years his senior – no one expected it to work.

Disraeli was a figure of violent controversy during his lifetime and for decades after; but whether he was opportunist or genius, adventurer or idealist, it is by now clear that he was the effective shaper of the modern Tory party and put a stamp on it that has remained vivid and relevant for over a hundred years.

Great Unionist (Conservative) Rally at Queen's Hall, October 1924, just before victory over Ramsay MacDonald's Labour government. Stanley Baldwin carries a good luck horseshoe; Mrs Baldwin (far left) was chairman of the Party Organisation.

Declaration of poll in Baldwin's constituency in the General Election of 1929. Prime Ministers fight for their constituency seat in an election just like all other MPs. Baldwin won here in Bewdley, but the Conservatives lost the election. In 1906 Arthur Balfour as PM actually lost his own seat.

Stanley Baldwin as PM, in 1925, in the garden at Chequers, the country house kept for British Prime Ministers. Baldwin had just won an election on a populist platform the papers dubbed the 'New Conservatism'.

Lord Salisbury

(Robert Cecil, 3rd Marquess of
Salisbury) 1830–1903

Member of Parliament 1853, went to
Lords 1868
Leader of the party 1884–1902
Prime Minister 1885 (June–
November), 1886–92, 1895–1902

THE MARQUESS of Salisbury, when he was Lord Cranborne, stalked out of the Disraeli–Derby cabinet in protest against giving the vote to the working class. Yet he was destined to benefit more than any other Conservative leader from the enlarged electorate, winning three general elections out of five and serving as Prime Minister for $13\frac{1}{2}$ years, longer than any other modern leader.

Aloof, pessimistic, deeply religious, Salisbury seems curiously out of tune with his age, the 'naughty nineties' – a time of bawdy music halls and raucous jingoism. But he was an adroit politician who led the party with great skill for seventeen years. He staved off the attempted coup by Randolph Churchill and managed to contain and even exploit the charismatic Liberal convert Joe Chamberlain. According to his daughter, he stopped at Central Office almost nightly after the Lords rose, to discuss party affairs with the Chief Agent Richard Middleton.

Salisbury surrounded himself personally and politically with his relatives, the aristocratic, intellectual and powerful Cecils (one MP, G.C.T. Bartley, put paid to his career by declaiming against the number of Lord Salisbury's relations in the government), but he still had a shrewd understanding of democratic political realities: 'To those who have found breakfast with difficulty,' he said in 1881, 'and do not know where to find dinner, intricate questions of politics are a matter of comparatively secondary interest.'

He also had a rare and underestimated quality of political courage. The American President Harry Truman defined it when he said, 'The buck stops here.' Lord Salisbury said it more elegantly: 'Those who have the absolute power of preventing lamentable events, and, knowing what is taking place, refuse to exercise that power, are responsible for what happens.'

Arthur Balfour

(1st Earl of Balfour) 1848–1930

Member of Parliament 1885–1906,
1906–1922
Leader of the party 1902–11
Prime Minister 1902–05

ARTHUR BALFOUR's brains are not in doubt, but his skill as a tactical politician may be. When he 'inherited' the premiership from his uncle Lord Salisbury in 1902, he saw with unflinching clarity Britain's exposed position in a dangerous world and took steps to remedy it, with international alliances to improve security and an Education Act to improve industrial competitiveness.

But he misjudged the potency of popular democracy and by wilfully neglecting working class interests (notably in the anti-union Taff Vale case and resistance to welfare legislation) he sowed the seeds of his party's and his own (he actually lost his seat) electoral debacle in 1906.

He also misjudged the depth of the divide separating the party's free traders from the protectionists (the same issue that undid Peel) and by trying to paper over the crack split the party yet again.

During the years in opposition he dismayed moderate opinion by encouraging the Tory-dominated House of Lords in their obstruction of social reform, obstruction that culminated in the dramatic emasculation of the second chamber by the Parliament Act 1911.

Balfour's hobby was philosophy, and his best known book was *A Defence of Philosophic Doubt*; but elegant intellects have limited appeal to mass electorates, and also (judging by Balfour's experience) to Parliamentary colleagues too. Balfour was forced out of the leadership in 1911, but remained influential in the upper reaches of the party until well into the 1920s.

Neville Chamberlain's war cabinet, November 1939. Churchill, so long in the political wilderness, joined the cabinet on 1st September. He wrote of his meeting with Chamberlain that afternoon: 'He invited me to become a member of the War Cabinet. I agreed to his proposal without comment, and on this basis we had a long talk on men and measures.'

1st November 1956, Sir Anthony Eden on his way to lunch with the Queen and then to face an ordeal in the House of Commons where the opposition was pressing censure of his government over the actions in Suez.

Andrew Bonar Law

1858–1923

Member of Parliament 1900–06,
    1906–10, 1911–23
Leader of the party 1911–21, 1922
    (October)–1923 (May)
Prime Minister 1922 (October)–
    1923 (May)

ANDREW BONAR LAW was 42 when he first entered Parliament in 1900, an obscure Scottish businessman with a 'thin and unmusical' voice, a blunt style and a glum outlook. Within eleven years he was the leader of the party, a 'dark horse' contender left unexpectedly standing in the winner's circle when Austen Chamberlain and Walter Long withdrew, fearing their impending clash would demolish an already demoralised party.

For nearly ten years Law led the party, first in opposition, then in the Liberal war-inspired coalition, but in 1921, when the ultimate office seemed almost within his grasp, illness forced him to resign. In 1922 the party conflict over whether to continue the coalition brought him back, and he won the premiership at last, although the pro-coalitionists (most of the cabinet and 'all the talent') held aloof and would not join his government. A bare seven months later cancer of the throat forced his resignation yet again.

He presided, during his term as leader, over the final formal merger of the Liberal Unionists and the Conservatives in 1912, and also over the slow reshaping of the party's character and image. The recalcitrant Die-Hards (as they called themselves) were gradually isolated and the moderates gained influence.

The one election manifesto Law wrote as Conservative leader reflected his own brand of sober conservatism: 'The nation's first need, in every walk of life, is to get on with its own work, with the minimum of interference at home and disturbance.'

Austen Chamberlain

1863–1937

Member of Parliament 1892–1914,
    1914–37
Leader of the party 1921–22

AUSTEN CHAMBERLAIN is the only Conservative leader this century who never became Prime Minister – although three times the prize was nearly his. Sandwiched historically between his brilliant erratic father Joe and his more famous half-brother Neville, Austen is remembered by his contemporaries in phrases like 'the perfect gentleman of politics' or, more cruelly, 'He always played the game – and he always lost it.'

In 1911 he stepped back from the fight for the leadership in order to preserve the unity of the party; in 1922 he resigned the leadership for the same reason. In 1923 he refused the dying Bonar Law's invitation to join the cabinet and become the heir apparent, feeling the party could not rally to him so soon after the bitter battle over the coalition.

Recalling his Liberal Unionist father's successful liaison with the Tories, he tried hard to permanently cement the Liberal–Conservative wartime coalition. He actually wrote to the Liberal Prime Minister Lloyd George in January 1922: 'My object has been to lead the Unionist Party [as the Conservative Party was then often called] to accept merger in a new Party under the lead of the present Prime Minister . . . so as to secure the widest and closest possible union of all men and women of constitutional and progressive views.'

But such non-partisanship has never been popular with the Conservative rank and file, who prefer their politics in bold colours, and in October 1922 the historic Carlton Club meeting voted Austen's coalition policy down, and he immediately resigned. In speaking to the MPs that morning, he gave a neat summary of the position of a Tory leader: 'It is you, deriving your authority from the electors, who conferred my authority upon me and made me what I am, and in such a matter as this I can accept no appeal from you to any other authority than that of the electors who are the masters of us all.'

The first television party political broadcast, 17th May 1955. Before the cameras at the BBC Lime Grove studios are (left to right) Iain Macleod (Minister of Health), R.A. Butler (Chancellor of the Exchequer), Sir Anthony Eden (PM), Harold Macmillan (Foreign Secretary) and Sir Walter Monckton (Minister of Labour). Nine days later the Conservatives won the election.

Harold Macmillan, as Prime Minister in August 1959, tours Basildon in Essex, one of the new towns created while he was Minister of Housing under Churchill.

It seems true, as the historian Sir Ivor Jennings wrote, that (at least with regard to its leaders), 'The Conservative party has hardly ever been conservative . . .'

As British society has changed, so has the style of its leaders. Peel, head of a government elected when only 7% of the adult population had the vote, was both proud and shy, and appeared to many arrogant and cold ('His smile is like the silver on a coffin lid,' said a contemporary unkindly). Yet he commanded immense respect by his statesmanship, integrity and prodigious hard work.

Harold Macmillan, more than a century later, had to appeal to a country where nearly every adult could vote. He was also one of the first to appeal to them over television. His witty stylish self-assurance so suited the new medium that cartoonists dubbed him 'The Entertainer'.

By contrast, Stanley Baldwin, who led the party in the 1920s and 1930s, projected a kind of stodgy calm that seemed to sooth his troubled times. 'Good old Stanley' his followers called him.

Some leaders adored their role: Disraeli called politics 'the great game' and played it with zest and consummate skill. Others did not: Lord Salisbury saw politics as 'slippery intrigues and abortive stratagems' and his own Prime Ministerial role as 'no higher than a policeman, whose utility would disappear if there were no criminals'.

However disparate they appear, the most successful leaders have had one thing in common: they have dominated the House of Commons. Even before the coming of the formal election procedure, the leader's

Stanley Baldwin

(1st Earl Baldwin of Bewdley)
1867–1947

Member of Parliament 1908–37
Leader of the party 1923–37
Prime Minister 1923 (6 months),
1924–29, (of national
government) 1935–37

STANLEY BALDWIN had only been Conservative leader and Prime Minister a few months when he dumbfounded his colleagues by calling an election – despite a secure parliamentary majority. They were even more appalled when he lost it, and let in Britain's first socialist government. But Baldwin was sanguine, and when he led the party to a triumphant victory less than a year later, he allowed it to be said he had planned it all along.

The public loved him (they came in tens of thousands to hear him speak): his image of decent honest trustworthiness, combined with a pipe and a fondness for pigs, was precisely what the people wanted in a politician in the 1920s. In many respects, however, it was not what their problems needed, and when events revealed it, he was reviled with a passion unparalleled since Peel.

In the two giant crises of his career Baldwin came up trumps: the General Strike (Macmillan, a new young MP at the time, said, 'I have always believed that it was Baldwin who saved the country from a real disaster in 1926') and the abdication of Edward VIII, when his 'simple skills', according to his critical biographer, saved the monarchy. But he could not succeed in resolving the long term problems of the time: unemployment, economic decline and the menace of Germany.

The popular press in 1924–25 called Baldwin's policies the 'New Conservatism', and certainly under him the party changed, accepting a massive dose of social reform legislation and reconciling itself (not without reluctance) to the retreat from Empire. 'You are not going to beat Labour,' he lectured the party faithful in 1924, 'on a policy of tranquillity, negation or sitting still.' His personal political creed, which he consistently tried to apply, he summed up in 1925: 'There is only one thing which I feel is worth giving one's whole strength to, and that is the binding together of all classes of our people in an effort to make life in this country better in every sense of the word. That is the end and object of my life in politics.'

Neville Chamberlain

1869–1940

Member of Parliament 1918–40
Leader of the party 1937–40
Prime Minister 1937–40

'MY CAREER is broken,' wrote Neville Chamberlain upon becoming an MP. 'How can a man of nearly 50, entering the House with this stigma upon him [his poor record as Director General of National Service] hope to achieve anything?'

In the event, of course, he achieved not only the premiership, but a truly remarkable record of progressive social reform. As Minister of Health under Baldwin and then Chancellor of the Exchequer in the National Government he created a 'circle of security' with legislation that included health insurance, pensions for widows and orphans, slum clearance, subsidised housing, the reform of the Poor Laws, and local government reorganisation.

But sadly, and with consummate irony, his career ended with a far greater stigma: the picture of Neville Chamberlain the world remembers is not the energetic effective social reformer: it is that fateful photograph of him upon his return from Munich, holding aloft the infamous pact with Hitler and declaring it meant 'Peace in our time'.

Within a year the holocaust had begun, and Chamberlain was in despair: 'Everything that I have worked for, everything that I have hoped for, everything that I have believed in during my public life, has crashed in ruins.' In May 1940 the House of Commons, in a dramatic vote, rejected him and his policies, and in six months more he was dead.

The old master has some advice for the new leader: Harold Macmillan on his 83rd birthday talks to Margaret Thatcher at the Carlton Club.

Sir Winston Churchill

1874–1965

Member of Parliament 1900–04,
   1906–08, 1908–18, 1918–22,
   1924–31, 1931–45, 1945–64
Leader of the party 1940–55
Prime Minister 1940–45 (National
   Coalition); 1951–55

THE GIGANTIC figure of
Winston Churchill stands astride
the century as well as the party;
his thunderous rhetoric echoes
down the generations and can still
prickle the flesh. As war leader
and Prime Minister of a national
coalition government, he became
such a huge national symbol of
courage and tenacity that the long
years before as a party politician
are obscured.

But had there been no war (and
Churchill himself called it 'the
unnecessary war') how would he
be viewed? Baldwin, who made
him Chancellor in 1924, said in
1943, 'The furnace of the war has
smelted out all the base metals in
him.'

From a party point of view he
had a chequered past: he changed
his party twice (Conservative to
Liberal in 1904, Liberal to Conservative in 1924). His grandson
said he viewed parties as horses in
a stable: you rode the one best
suited to the task. As Chancellor
of the Exchequer in the 1920s he
made some bad decisions (notably
the return to the Gold Standard);
as the pugnacious editor of the
government newspaper during
the General Strike he did not
altogether follow Baldwin's low-
key lead. He broke with the party
over India in 1930, taking a die-
hard stance against any move
towards self-government, and
thus spent nearly a decade in the
political wilderness, a lonely
looming figure, issuing magnificent prescient, but largely
unheeded warnings against
Hitler.

Yet in the end, as A.J.P. Taylor
has said, he was 'twice the instrument of destiny: once when he
inspired Great Britain to survive
as an independent power and
again when he brought Soviet
Russia into the comity of
nations'. Inspire Britain he
unquestionably did, and when
'this island race' stood isolated
there are many who claim his
words alone sustained it.

Then in 1945 the same island
race rejected him and his party
and installed the first Labour government to command a working
majority. Raymond Mortimer, a
journalist, wrote then: 'Our debt
to him is probably greater than to
any other politician in our history, but I could not feel on that
account any obligation to vote for
him.' Evidently much of the
country felt the same: Labour
under Attlee had a majority of
180. Churchill, however, never
would surrender, and in 1951 he
became Prime Minister again, at
nearly 77, and presided over the
first years of what was to be one
of the longest and most successful
Conservative administrations.

position was dependent on the support of Conservative MPs. Hard-
hitting speeches at the dispatch box, preferably ones that demoralised the
opposition, were essential to keep that support. Even the restrained Peel
wrote to his wife with satisfaction about the 'flagellation' he gave
Palmerston in the House. But if the dominance wavered – as it did with
Anthony Eden after Suez – the leader was in trouble. Eden's dispatch-box
performance in the Suez crisis was 'Deplorable!' according to a contemporary journalist, Ian Waller. In it 'Sir Anthony suffered a blow to his
prestige that was clearly reflected in the silent devastated ranks of the
Conservative benches behind him.'

But when a leader does dominate the House the effect is electrifying: Sir
William Fraser, MP for Kidderminster, after listening to Disraeli, was
obviously overcome, though powerless to describe it: 'No one who has
not [heard him] can form any idea of his powers. His speeches when read
give no adequate idea of their effect. The impact made on an emotional
assembly like the House of Commons can never be put into print.'

Churchill, of course, dominated the House as no other politician has
before or since. Harold Nicolson MP described his performance in the

The House of Commons, 1833.
National Portrait Gallery, London.

Chatsworth House, Derbyshire, home of
the Dukes of Devonshire.

The lobby of the House of Commons, 1886. Joe Chamberlain (with the monocle) and Lord Randolph Churchill (with the top-hat and the buttonhole) are among the group in the centre. Vanity Fair *cartoon.*

Hatfield House, Hertfordshire, home of the Marquesses of Salisbury.

Sir Alec Douglas-Home as PM in October 1963 in the Cabinet Room at 10 Downing St. following Macmillan's resignation. Despite the struggle for the leadership, all the Macmillan cabinet agreed to serve under Sir Alec save two: Iain Macleod and Enoch Powell.

Sir Anthony Eden

(1st Lord Avon) 1897–1977

Member of Parliament 1923–61
Leader of the party 1955–57
Prime Minister 1955–57

ANTHONY EDEN – distinguished, elegant, holder of the Military Cross for valour in the First World War – was an excellent Foreign Secretary, the youngest for 150 years. For 30 years before he finally reached the premiership he practised diplomacy at the highest levels. So it is remarkable that his career foundered and was wrecked – spectacularly – on an issue of foreign policy.

For fifteen years Eden had been Churchill's heir apparent. The succession, when it finally came, was almost monarchical: no one questioned it, and Eden was even married to Churchill's niece.

He had been an anti-appeaser in the 1930s (Chamberlain forced his resignation from the Foreign Office because of it), and his conviction that Hitler could have been stopped cast a long shadow down the years, influencing his precipitate action against Nasser's takeover of the Suez canal. International opinion recoiled, domestic opinion was divided: 'the debates in the House of Commons reached a degree of emotional intensity not seen since the days of Irish Home Rule.' Then suddenly, after the cease-fire, but while British troops were still in Egypt, Eden (on doctor's orders) left and went to Jamaica for several weeks.

Even before Suez his position had been shaky ('irresolute', 'arrogant', 'interfering' his colleagues call him in their memoirs), and although his health recovered his reputation did not, and on 9th January 1957 he resigned.

Oddly, history has revalued the man, although not the event. The Suez affair is still seen as a humiliating disaster, but Eden is viewed by many as a gallant tragic figure, crushed by inexorable events.

The Oxford Union: fertile seedbed for Conservative leaders. The speaker in this December 1938 debate is Edward Heath.

Harold Macmillan

1894–

Member of Parliament 1924–63
Leader of the party 1957–63
Prime Minister 1957–63

HAROLD MACMILLAN wrote that, upon reading Disraeli's biography in 1912, his reaction was, 'If Dizzy had made himself leader of a party and Prime Minister by his own unaided effort, could I not have a go?'

Forty-five years later he made it. But when he did the party and the country were in post-Suez disarray, the economy was weak, and Britain's world role was diminished and unclear. Within three years Macmillan had revived the party, restored national morale, re-stimulated the economy (a matter of controversy), and reconciled much of the country to its post-imperial role. 'The man's a genius,' said Harold Wilson in exasperation. When a cartoonist attacked him with a drawing labelled 'SuperMac' everyone thought the name a perfect fit. Under him in 1959 the Conservatives won their third victory in a row, with an increased majority of 100 seats.

Macmillan's style was inimitable: cool, casual, confident – 'unflappable', Lord Hailsham called it. Once while he was delivering an important speech at the UN Khrushchev (the Russian Premier) took off his shoe and began banging it on the table. Macmillan calmly remarked: 'I'd like that translated if I may.'

But the style was also inseparable from the success, and when the self-assurance slipped following by-election defeats in 1961, there was trouble. In an attempt to brighten the government with new faces he sacked seven cabinet ministers at once (the 'night of the long knives'). The Gallup Poll recorded his popularity instantly sunk to 36%. Even more damaging was the veto of Britain's application to join the EEC. 'It was Macmillan's ace,' said a Central Office official, 'and De Gaulle trumped it.' He resigned, unexpectedly through illness, in October 1963.

The influences of his youth – his Christian Socialist grandfather, Liberal Unionist father and his own experiences of the depression – marked him deeply, and there were always critics on the party's right wing who thought him 'soft'. He himself said, 'during the early part of my life I was accused of leaning too much to the Left. I have seen recently accusations that I leaned too far to the Right. I propose, as I have always, to follow the Middle Way.'

Sir Alec Douglas-Home

(Lord Home of The Hirsel) 1903–

Member of Parliament 1931–45, 1950–51 (went to Lords), returned to Commons 1963–74
Leader of the party 1963–65
Prime Minister 1963–64

SIR ALEC DOUGLAS-HOME was Prime Minister less than a year – only Bonar Law had a briefer tenancy of No. 10 – and during virtually the whole time he was campaigning for the general election of October 1964 (in which to universal surprise he was only narrowly defeated).

He became leader, much to his own astonishment – 'the question of my succession to Macmillan had simply not crossed my mind' – in the scuffle following Macmillan's resignation. Harold Wilson made much capital out of his being the 14th Earl, until Home asked on television, 'Wasn't he the 14th Mr Wilson?' The gibes about the 50,000 acre Scottish estate were harder to deflect. In fact, before he could take Macmillan's place he had to renounce his ancient title (in the 19th century Lords could be Prime Ministers, but not now), and win a constituency by-election. He had been in Parliament many years; served as Neville Chamberlain's PPS before the war, and as Foreign Secretary under Macmillan, but it was 12 years since he had been in the Commons. 'I was quite unprepared,' he said, 'for the sheer impact of noise after the quiet and civilised proceedings of the House of Lords; and if it had not been for the solid table between me and the Opposition I should have been seen to be shaking at the knees.'

His leadership began in an atmosphere of sourness – it was all fixed by the 'Magic Circle of old Etonians', said Ian Macleod, who refused to serve under him – but it turned to one of great affection as Home so visibly embodied traits the Conservative party has traditionally admired: courage under fire (he was mercilessly barracked during the campaign and once physically attacked); good sportsmanship (he cheerfully accepted a subordinate position under his successor, Heath), and a sense of humour. His major legacy to the party was to set up the formal machinery for electing the leader. Having set it up, he gracefully resigned and let it be used.

Edward Heath conducts the London Symphony Orchestra to mark the publication of his second book Music: a Joy for Life, *1976.*

Edward Heath

1916–

Member of Parliament 1950–
Leader of the party 1965–74
Prime Minister 1970–74

EDWARD HEATH is the only Conservative leader whose extra-parliamentary activities gained nearly as much public attention as his political ones. While Leader of the Opposition he became famous as an international yachtsman, and won the Sydney to Hobart Race in 1969. Then while Prime Minister, in 1971, he captained the winning British Admiral's Cup team. He was almost equally renowned as a musician, and pictures of him playing, singing and conducting appeared nearly as often as ones of him speaking.

He was the first Conservative leader to be elected by a ballot of MPs – and the first to be deposed by one. When he became Prime Minister in June 1970 he was, at 54, the youngest Conservative Premier since Peel, and had a reputation for courage, tenacity and tactical skill, earned during a long tenure as Chief Whip. His outstanding achievement as Prime Minister was to secure Britain's entry into the EEC, a goal he had pursued ever since he led the first Common Market negotiating team in the early 1960s. But much of his administration was marked by controversy, and it ended in the 'confrontation' with the miners and the highly unpopular three-day week.

Heath was greatly admired in the Parliamentary party for his competence and prodigious grasp of complicated briefs (he often spoke for over an hour without a note, without a flaw), but he was not greatly loved. Nigel Fisher MP wrote of him: 'To acquaintances he is impenetrable, and most of us who have served in Parliament with him for more than a quarter of a century feel we know him no better today than when we first met.' But to Douglas Hurd, Heath's Political Secretary throughout the administration, and later MP for Mid-Oxon, he was 'A most remarkable Patriot and Prime Minister'.

vote of confidence debate in 1942, during the darkest months of the war: 'When he reaches his peroration he ceases to be genial and becomes emphatic. He crouches over the box and strikes it. "It only remains for us to act. I offer no apologies. I offer no excuses. I make no promises. In no way have I mitigated the sense of danger and impending misfortunes that hang over us. But at the same time I avow my confidence, never stronger than at this moment, that we shall bring this conflict to an end in a manner agreeable to the interests of our country and the future of the world. I have finished." (Then that downward sweep of the two arms, with the palms open to receive the stigmata.) "Let every man act now in accordance with what he thinks is his duty in harmony with his heart and conscience." It takes a long time to count the votes, and finally they are recorded as 464 to 1.'

There is at least one other thing Conservative leaders have in common. It is their attempts, with varying degrees of success, to conform to Edmund Burke's standard of a statesman as one who combines 'a disposition to preserve' with an 'ability to improve'.

Peel, as Prime Minister in 1842, during one of the great reforming administrations of the century, said his daily 'practical problem' was 'to harmonise as far as possible the satisfaction of new wants and necessities with the framework of time-honoured institutions . . .'

Disraeli, as Prime Minister in 1868, shortly after doubling the electorate with the second Reform Act, said, 'In a progressive country change is constant, and the great question is not whether you should resist change, which is inevitable, but whether that change should be carried out in deference to the manners, the customs, the laws and the traditions of a people . . .'

Stanley Baldwin, leader of the party for fourteen years, said, 'The responsibility – and it is a great responsibility – that rests with a leader is to try and adapt the policy according to the deep-laid foundations of the party principles to meet whatever may come in this world.'

Edward Heath, as Prime Minister in 1972, taking Britain along the unknown road into Europe, restated the theme with modern succinctness: 'We are going to build on the past, but we are not going to be strangled by it.'

It is this theme, more than any other, that has consistently characterised Conservative leaders: their desire to have change come by evolution, not revolution, and their desire to preserve the essence of ancient British institutions and values while adapting them to a changing world.

Margaret and Denis Thatcher move into 10 Downing St., Friday 4th May 1979, within hours of the Conservative election victory. Mrs Thatcher formed her entire administration – 98 members – over the weekend.

Margaret Thatcher

1926–

Member of Parliament 1959–
Leader of the party 1975–
Prime Minister 1979–

'To ME it is like a dream,' said Margaret Thatcher when the MPs' votes for the leadership were counted in February 1975, 'that the next name in the list after Harold Macmillan, Sir Alec Douglas-Home and Edward Heath is Margaret Thatcher.'

She was not the only one who was surprised. For a perceptible period there was a sensation of stunned silence in the country that the Conservatives – the party always caricatured as old-fashioned, fuddy-duddy and overwhelmingly male – had chosen a woman as its leader. It was an amazement repeated world-wide four years later when the British electorate made her Prime Minister, by the largest margin of votes – a clear 7% – achieved by any victorious party since 1935.

This was not, however, the first remarkable thing Margaret Thatcher had done. She grew up above a grocery shop in a small Lincolnshire town; she went early to Oxford, at 17, studied chemistry and became President of the Conservative Association. Later, married and pregnant, she studied for and passed the Bar exam, and during the same year gave birth to twins. ('Let's face it,' said Jill Tweedie in the *Guardian*, 'any woman who can have two children from one pregnancy is obviously more efficient than the rest of us.')

But it was not her sex that made the choice of Margaret Thatcher as Conservative leader and then Prime Minister truly radical: it was her clearly stated commitment to totally change the direction of post-war Britain by reducing the role of government and restoring a free-market economy to reinvigorate individual initiative. The Conservatives, under her leadership, ran their 1979 campaign on a platform unusual in its explicitness, and therefore took the definitive victory to be a mandate.

Margaret Thatcher constructed her entire government over the weekend after the election, telephoning even the most junior ministers herself, and began business immediately the following week. A bare four months later the international magazine *The Economist* said, 'She has stamped her personal mark on her administration more firmly than any prime minister since the war. She has set in train the reversal of state socialism which was her ambition in government.'

Black Rod, before the Mace in the House of Commons begins the ancient ritual that opens Parliament, leading MPs to the House of Lords to hear the Queen's Speech outlining the new government's legislative programme. Margaret Thatcher, sitting in the PM's place in front of the dispatch box, is flanked by her chief Ministers: (right to left) Sir Geoffrey Howe, William Whitelaw, Norman St John Stevas.

CHAPTER 2
The MPs

THE PHYSICAL surroundings of an MP's job have changed hardly at all from the 1850s to the 1980s, but the job itself has altered dramatically.

The centre of action is still the small debating chamber, where Government and Opposition face each other across a space just too wide for a sword thrust to hit home. Leaders sit on the front benches, ordinary members on the back (hence 'back benchers'). The clash of debate is no rowdier now than then (although hearing it over the radio for the first time has startled many listeners). In fact, the House is actually more decorous now: a new MP in 1833 was scandalised by the behaviour and wrote, 'If the public could nightly see all that passes within our walls, I fear the reverence now so rife towards our respected selves would be woefully diminished . . . around and about, overhead in the galleries, on the floor, lying at full length on the benches, talking, laughing, hooting, coughing, sleeping, are to be seen the members . . . confusion, riot . . . groans and braying, are the order of the day. One member possesses the faculty of hooting like an owl, to the great disturbance of the gravity of the assembly, and evident annoyance of the Speaker.'

Outside the chamber the atmosphere of Parliament remains that of a select Victorian men's club: panelled walls, smoking rooms, deep leather chairs, book-lined libraries, stimulating discussion and rich political gossip.

Rituals remain unchanged as well: the annual session is opened by the Monarch, resplendently robed, arriving in a golden coach. Each daily session is opened with a file of men in powdered wigs and knee breeches, with Black Rod in the lead, carrying the ceremonial Mace.

But behind the pageantry and ceremonial procedures, whose roots go

Within minutes of a vote (division) being called MPs must be physically present in the voting lobbies or their vote is lost. The sprint to the lobby shown here in a drawing from 1856 still goes on today.

The 1832 Reform Act was the effective beginning of the modern Parliament, with MPs starting to be accountable to an electorate incorporating the male middle class. The Conservatives resisted the reforms at first, but swiftly and pragmatically adapted after they were passed.

Sir Richard Cross MP, Disraeli's sagacious Home Secretary, and a representative of the middle classes who flocked to the Tories in the 1860s and 1870s and gradually replaced the country squires as the dominant factor in the party. Cross was a very popular Home Secretary; the street crowds sang this jingle about him:

> For he's a jolly good fellow
> Whatever the Rads may think
> For he has shortened the hours of work
> And lengthened the hours of drink.

Disraeli's maiden speech in the House of Commons, from a contemporary drawing. This first speech was a disaster, drowned, according to an observer, in 'hisses, groans, hoots, catcalls, drumming with feet, loud conversation and imitation of animals.' Undeterred, Disraeli eventually rose to the top primarily by the power of his tongue.

back seven hundred years, the work of MPs today is quite unlike their predecessors a century ago. A backbench MP in the early 1800s had a leisured, undemanding life. Not much was expected of government beyond defence of the realm: Parliament only sat from February to July, and even an assiduous member need attend only three days a week – after dinner. A backbencher had only the most distant control over the government of the day, and as he was unpaid and his electorate was small and unrepresentative (in 1832 only one man in seven had a vote) he did not consider his constituents had any but the most distant control over him.

Today much is expected of government: Parliament sits from October to August (with Christmas, Easter and Whitsun breaks); some 2000 pages are being added to the statute book every year; the backbencher is expected by his electorate to both influence policy, control the government and deal with a multitude of constituents' problems as well. The average Conservative backbencher receives at least one hundred pieces of mail a week (some receive far more), holds 'surgeries' for constitutents' problems, serves on Conservative committees shaping party policy and Parliamentary committees shaping legislation. He is expected to regularly attend debates in the chamber, where his presence and performance are monitored by his local association and the local press. ('The trouble all began,' said one MP plaintively, 'when they began printing the Division [voting] lists in 1836 . . .')

The change in the nature of the job is reflected in the changed kind of Conservative MPs; in the last century many Tories entered Parliament out of family tradition, a sense of public duty, or for the undeniable glamour and prestige (in the absence of much other entertainment politics then excited intense interest, and the great figures were national celebrities).

The Ladies' Gallery in the House of Commons. In the early 19th century women were totally excluded from the Chamber, but after 1834 a maximum of 24 were allowed to watch debates from this specially screened gallery. An unseemly outburst of applause, however, in 1888, caused them to be barred altogether until 1909. The trelliswork screen was finally removed in 1918, when women got the vote, and they were allowed to sit in any part of the Strangers' Gallery.

Above left *Walter Long MP, a country squire of ancient lineage, symbolised the old 19th-century 'Country Party' in the 1911 leadership contest. But the Tories were no longer the party of the landed gentry, and Bonar Law, a Glasgow iron merchant, became leader.*

Above right *W.H. Smith MP, a pillar of the Victorian bourgeoisie, whom Disraeli first elevated to high office in the party and the government to counterbalance the heavy weight of Tory country squires and aristocracy. Smith became Leader of the House of Commons, and was nicknamed, without malice, 'Old Morality'. This photo dates from 1889; he died in 1891.*

Nancy, Lady Astor, arrives at Parliament in 1919, the first woman MP to take her seat in the House of Commons, and the only one until 1922. She is wearing what became known as her 'uniform': chic black suit with white collar and cuffs and black tricorne hat. Harold Macmillan remembers that when she spoke 'there was always some anxiety into what pitfall she might be enticed either by her own enthusiasm or by a well-timed interruption.'

F.E. Smith MP (later Lord Birkenhead) speaking to a rally in 1912. Unlike Disraeli, F.E. Smith's maiden speech was a triumph and gave him a national reputation overnight; but it did not subsequently survive his support of the die-hard Unionist peers, his stand on Irish Home Rule and his unbridled opposition to women's votes.

Walter Long, contender for the leadership in 1911, described the typical Conservative backbencher a hundred years ago: 'The average country gentleman entered the House of Commons in much the same way that I did, performing what he regarded as his duty, without any particular ambition to do more than serve his county and his country, and the agriculturist interests to the best of his ability. He was content to be present in the afternoon, and, when required, after dinner, to record a vote if there was a division, but otherwise to take no active part in the proceedings . . .'

Then, as successive Reform Acts enlarged the electorate, people with a vote to bestow began to expect more of their government and their MPs, and the job became more demanding: 'The House of Commons has lost much of its old attractiveness,' grumbled the Member for West Surrey in 1883. 'The duties of a member become yearly more engrossing. It is not only that the hours of work are longer than they were and attendance more trying, but constituencies are much more exacting. The recess is far from being a holiday . . .'

As the work load increased and the social cachet declined, men stopped entering Parliament for the glamour or from a sense of duty, and more from a determination to accomplish things. For a while the old style and the new existed side by side: 'Young man, you are always going to your Constituency,' said an older MP to the young Alec Douglas-Home. 'I replied that I was wont to go about once a fortnight, and enquired how often he visited Greenock. His reply was, "Oh, about five times in thirty years".'

In the early years after the 1832 Reform Act candidates often chose themselves – men of independent means and independent mind, with perhaps family connections in the area, would declare themselves a contender for the seat. Often they were not opposed: in 1841, for instance, over half the seats were uncontested, although this did not necessarily make it any cheaper to run (see page 65). If a constituency needed a Conservative candidate, Robert Peel's fledgling party organisation, operating from the Carlton Club in London, would supply one.

Today, Conservative Central Office maintains a more formal list of hopeful candidates, chosen by a selection panel from hundreds of applications every year. As the job of MP has become more serious, the selection panel now increasingly looks for people of professional competence and some political experience: local councillors, officers and activists in local associations. Unlike in Peel's day (and even into the 20th century), they no longer have to look for people with financial assets. Party reforms made after the Second World War include one forbidding a Conservative candidate or MP to contribute more than £25 (now upped to £100) a year

The candidate's committee room: Alfred Bossom talks to his Agent in Maidstone before the February 1950 election.

Patricia Hornsby-Smith visits a Kent pig farm in the run-up to the February 1950 election. She won the seat.

to local party funds. This reform was not before time. In 1924 Baldwin had told the party: 'An old tradition – and a very bad tradition it is today – still prevails in too many parts of the country. It is that the first thing a constituency has to do is to look for a member who will carry the association on his back, and who will subscribe to everything in the division – and, when they have got that, they do not much mind what else they have got. Now that was never a good thing; it is a particularly bad thing today.'

Removing the financial hurdles for candidates was a key factor in opening up the range of people who could fight as Conservatives and has had an important impact on the nature of the Parliamentary party.

When a local constituency association needs a Conservative candidate they set up a selection committee who can consult the Central Office list (they do not have to) and choose from it people to interview. The selection committee may see fifty or even 100 hopefuls before choosing a short list of perhaps five to appear before the full constituency association. The average membership of a local Conservative Association is several thousand; several hundred usually attend this selection meeting, where the final five (or so) make speeches and answer questions, and where a vote is taken to decide the association's official candidate.

Florence Horsbrugh MP, Minister of Education, admires a student's costume while opening a new LCC Technical College in 1952. An MP's elevation from backbench to Minister depends wholly on the leader of the party.

Conservative associations in recent years have shown a consistent preference for people with experience in law, industry and commerce, with a university degree, a fairly high standard of speaking ability, and at least some local political experience. The composition of the Parliamentary party reflects these preferences. Country squires have become quite rare.

A Conservative candidate, once selected and elected, often sits for the constituency for the rest of his political life. The relationship between the MP and his association is therefore not unlike a marriage, and has its own internal tensions – not least the question of whether he is their representative or their delegate. In 1774, Edmund Burke MP, addressing his own electors in Bristol, announced firmly for the former, and his words have been used as a touchstone by Conservative MPs for over 200 years: 'Your representative owes you not his industry only, but his

Reg Prentice MP (left) campaigning with candidate Vivian Bendall in a 1978 by-election. Reg Prentice, a former Labour Minister, left the Labour party in 1977, then fought and won as a Conservative in 1979, when he was made a Minister of State in the Thatcher administration.

judgment, and he betrays, instead of serving you, if he sacrifices it to your opinion . . . To deliver an opinion is the right of all men; and that of constituents is a weighty and respectable opinion, which a representative ought always to rejoice to hear, and which he ought always most seriously to consider. But *authoritative* instructions; *mandates* issued, which the member is bound blindly and implicitly to obey, to vote and argue for, though contrary to the clearest conviction of his judgment and conscience – these are things utterly unknown to the laws of this land, and which arise from a fundamental mistake of the whole order and tenor of our constitution.'

In other words, Tory MPs, although committing to carefully consider the opinions of their constituents, retain the right to act as their own judgment dictates.

Many Conservative MPs are content to remain as private members on the backbenches, acting as watchdogs over legislation, contributing to party policy through the advisory committees (there are always dozens of committees and sub-committees sitting studying policy options and examining the effects of legislation), and serving their constituents' interests. Many MPs are finding these interests are absorbing an ever larger part of their time, as government extends its control over ever larger parts of people's lives. Individuals increasingly need protection and redress against bureaucracy, and as Conservative MPs are ideologically biased toward individual freedom and against government control, they find themselves more and more acting as local ombudsmen and welfare officers. People the Council has evicted, parents who need special schooling for a handicapped child, prisoners' wives without support, people erroneously pursued by the taxman, people penalised by industrial tribunals . . . all these and more increasingly feel their avenue of redress is their MP. Often they are right.

The views of private Conservative members in Parliament are organised and transmitted to the leaders through the 1922 Committee. This was formed (in the year of its name) when a group of newly elected (and new style) MPs were astonished and appalled to discover no proper channels existed for backbenchers to communicate with the leadership. Party policies were simply announced, and MPs were expected then to defend them in public. The group formed the 1922 Committee to correct this. It now meets every week while Parliament is in session, and acts as a forum for backbench discussion of party policy. A Whip always attends and lets the leader know what the party is thinking.

If, however, a Conservative backbencher aspires to the front bench, there are several ways to get there, although none of them are fool-proof since even at the best of political times only 20–30% of the party's MPs can be accommodated in the government.

One route is for a member to reveal a flair for a particular subject and put it to work on a specialist committee. As early as 1881 Frederic Harrison was fulminating about the impossibility of understanding

A modern MP's job is often neither glamorous nor easy. This January 1979 photo shows Hugh Rossi, MP for Haringey, talking to one of the NUPE pickets who had closed a school in his constituency.

In the 19th century an MP might visit his constituency once every five years or so to count the poll. In the 20th they are more likely to visit once a week. Here John Moore, MP for a marginal seat, answers questions from future constituents.

modern legislation: 'The so-called Ministers . . . elaborate ingenious and complicated drafts for the House to consider: drafts usually too technical for the body of the House to understand . . . these drafts accumulate into incredible mountains of printed matter, encrusted with fresh mountains of inconsistent and impossible amendments. A few experts alone understand the effect of this pile of projects and counter-projects . . .'

Since some eighty years later the 'pile of projects' is even more complex, an MP versed in one of the more demanding disciplines (i.e. tax law, as Mrs Thatcher was) and willing to employ the expertise in the hard slog of a committee room is well placed for promotion.

The Whips Office (they are named after 'Whippers-In' – the gentlemen at a hunt responsible for keeping the hound pack in line), where Parliamentary business is scheduled and strategy decided, and the behaviour, opinions and peccadilloes of every member are carefully recorded, is a well-travelled route to the top. Edward Heath spent many years in the Whips Office.

Impressive Parliamentary performance can single out a private member, but it has to be pretty impressive. Disraeli and Churchill made their marks this way.

Some who have become Ministers started as a PPS (Personal Private Secretary – known rudely in the ranks as 'Dogsbody') to a Minister. This is the bottom rung of the ladder, and given a snake-free climb the PPS can make it to the top. Alec Douglas-Home was Neville Chamberlain's PPS.

A colourful rebellion or resignation, or a dramatic statement to press or television can catapult a private member into the public eye, but it is a dangerous ploy in a party where the leader makes all cabinet appointments. Churchill and Anthony Eden both had well-publicised resignations. So did Enoch Powell. Winston Churchill's father, Lord Randolph, attempted a spectacular resignation to gain a point and came a cropper when Lord Salisbury accepted it (see page 90).

Even without the dangers attendant on ambition, however, there are difficulties enough in the conditions of MPs. The dignified image of Parliament outside Westminster is curiously at odds with its actual working: it was 1896 when Augustine Birrell MP declared in the Chamber that 'Private Members had to live in the House under conditions which were well nigh intolerable!' Conditions today are virtually unchanged. The Chamber itself has seats for 437, although there are over 630 members – and have been for 200 years. The designer is said to have explained complacently that the inevitable squash during popular debates would add to the air of excitement, and the chamber would not look so embarrassingly empty during unpopular ones.

Votes must be registered by members physically walking through the 'Aye' or 'No' lobbies (long corridors that flank the Chamber). As soon as a vote (Division) is called a raucous bell begins to clang, and members have eight minutes to make the lobby before the doors are shut and locked. As the Palace of Westminster has two miles of corridors, fleetness of foot is an important skill. If a member is out of the precincts when an

Mr Speaker, in full wig, marches through the ornate Central Lobby of the Palace of Westminster every day to begin the Parliamentary debates. The electorate and the country may have been wholly transformed in 150 years, yet the Parliamentary rituals remain unchanged.

The Library at the House of Commons.

important Division is called he must make it back or face severe censure by his Whips. The Metropolitan Police have standing orders to keep the entrances clear, and strollers past Parliament are often startled by Honourable Members tumbling from taxis and sprinting full tilt toward the Chamber.

The House nominally sits from 2.30 in the afternoon until 10 at night on Mondays to Thursdays, and from 9.30 am to 2.30 pm on Fridays (committees in the mornings). But adjournment is nearly always postponed and debate continues into the small hours. If a private member wishes to speak in one of these debates, he can only 'try to catch the Speaker's eye', and show his earnestness by remaining on the benches throughout his colleagues' contributions, bounding hopefully to his feet at every change of speaker, though it means missing tea, dinner and the last bus home. To prepare for the debate, or indeed to conduct any other Parliamentary business, a member has no private office, only desk space for himself and his secretary, and a small school-style locker.

Despite all this (because of it?), the number of people wishing to be Tory MPs grows, not shrinks, and the morale of the Conservative members is consistently high. The intimate conditions appear to encourage friendship among colleagues, and the adversary conditions vis à vis the opposition encourage teamwork and a kind of esprit de corps. Very few voluntarily leave the job, some remaining until well into their seventies and eighties, and Conservative MPs suffering electoral defeat usually instantly apply to run again.

CHAPTER 3
The Rank and File

AT THE 1950 Conservative Conference (which was very crowded), a motion was put forward to reduce the number of delegates allowed to come to Conferences in the future. Speaking against it, a Mrs Joan Benton said: 'This is my first Conference. It has been the most exciting thing that has ever happened to me; and Mrs Benton wants to come again.'

Mrs Benton's enthusiasm must be shared by the majority of the Conservative party's grass roots membership – they must enjoy the party and its activities, for there are no tangible rewards, and for many there is a great deal of work. They – the grass roots membership – provide a major part of the party's funds and all of the electoral legwork. They work for the Conservative candidate in the local borough elections, regional county elections, general Parliamentary elections and European Parliamentary elections. They are responsible for selecting these candidates, for getting them into office (if they can) and in the long run for changing them if they do a poor job.

There are over 600 Conservative Associations in Great Britain, affiliated to the National Union of Conservative Associations. They owe their existence to the Reform Acts of the 19th century, and in particular to Disraeli's Act of 1867, since before there was mass voting there was no need of a mass party.

Primrose League gathering at Hatfield in 1896. Theoretically founded to honour Disraeli (it was named for his favourite flower) the League's social functions, elaborate costumes and resounding titles were a powerful lure that attracted a mass membership. Their electioneering for the Conservative party was discreet until 1895 when they openly campaigned.

Photo from the Hatfield family album labelled 'Headquarters Staff, Election July 15 1895'. Salisbury's influence undoubtedly shaped the modern party. 'What we want,' he told the National Union, 'is more discussion, more information, more light. The more light there is thrown on any political question, . . . the more certainty there is that they will steadily and surely verge to the Conservative cause.'

Lord Cranborne, Salisbury's eldest son, went off to the Boer War immediately following his election in 1900. His wife Alice wrote the thank-you notes. The cover, printed in colour, featured pictures of Lord Salisbury, Balfour and Joe Chamberlain, as well as Lord and Lady Cranborne. MPs' thank-you notes today are less lavish.

In Peel's time, the tiny electorate could be directly influenced by the candidate – either with high-minded persuasion or low-minded corruption – and the idea of mass parties appeared ridiculous. Indeed to Lord Stanley in 1835 it appeared downright dangerous: on being informed of a plan to form a Conservative Association for North Lancashire, he wrote in horror: 'Could the ingenuity of man suggest a source more certain to send forth . . . bitter waters, than the spirit which will be engendered by the establishment of your association? . . . I can conceive nothing more dangerous to public liberty, nothing more injurious to a stable or a rational Administration than such a state of things . . . two rival sets of political associations engaged in a deadly struggle with each other for the maintenance of extreme principles . . .'

But a bare 43 years later, Disraeli as Prime Minister was saying: 'nature is herself organisation; and if there were not a great directing force which controls and guides and manages everything, you would have nothing but volcanoes, earthquakes, and deluges. In public life without organisation similar effects would be produced . . . It is only by encouraging that spirit of discipline that you will be able to maintain yourself [he was talking to a deputation from local Conservative associations] in that power which you have now obtained and which is the most perfect answer to those who once sneered at Constitutional Associations . . .'

It was by then (1878) apparent to politicians of every colour that stable government in a democracy elected by anything approaching universal suffrage would be impossible without party organisation. The Conservatives, therefore, set to work to develop one, beginning promptly in the very year of the Reform Act, 1867, with the formation of the National Union. There were already a number of local Conservative or Constitutional associations, and the Union was formed (according to an early statement of its principles) 'for the purpose of effecting a systematic organisation of Conservative feeling and influence throughout the country, by helping in the formation and work of the Constitutional Associations which have so rapidly increased in numbers. It is notorious that the Constitutional cause has suffered much from the want of organisation amongst its supporters.'

The Union did not get off to a roaring start: at their first Conference in 1868 (forerunner of the one Mrs Benton so enjoyed) attendance totalled seven: six delegates and the chairman. But then, they had called it for four days after Christmas in Birmingham. By 1901, 800 came, and by 1970 6000.

The leadership of the party appreciated the work of the National Union rather mildly at first: in 1874 one of the delegates to the Conference said anxiously, 'I hope the members of the Government will not think of giving the cold shoulder to these Associations . . .' But their interest markedly intensified with the passage of the Corrupt Practices Act, 1883. This not only finally outlawed (and with effective enforcement) the bribing of voters (in case anyone was still considering it with an electorate enlarged to two million): it also limited campaign expenditure and severely restricted the number of paid political helpers a candidate could employ. Suddenly the voluntary party became extremely popular.

The purpose of the voluntary party, clearly stated from the beginning, has been to organise Conservative support in the country and get out the Conservative vote on election day. But early on, Lord Salisbury, one of the canniest Conservative leaders, who led from 1886 to 1902, warned fellow politicians not to forget a prime reason the voluntary party worked for them: 'The gratification to pride or pocket, whatever its amount may be, which is conferred by office, can only be the lot of a small fraction in

Bonar Law speaking to the annual Conference in Leeds, November 1911. Some delegates may have wondered who he was as he had been chosen leader only three days before by MPs at the Carlton Club.

Stanley and Mrs Baldwin arrive at the Guildhall in Worcester to say farewell to their constituents at the time of his resignation in 1937. Baldwin had a great respect for the party rank and file: 'Don't lose touch with your constituency,' he counselled new MPs in 1924, 'don't ever mistake the voice of the clubman and the voice of the Pressman in London for the voice of the country. It is the country which has returned you; it is the country which will judge you.'

*Winston Churchill addressing the
Conservative Conference in Empress
Hall, London, 1949. The leader's
speech is always the climax of the annual
Conference, invariably (in modern
times) received with a standing ovation
by upwards of 5000 representatives of
local associations.*

*Clementine Churchill urges on the
workers in her husband's election
headquarters in February 1950. The
Conservative rank and file – several
millions of them – are the ones who do
the constituency legwork and paperwork
at election time and in between.*

*Getting out the vote: Conservative
volunteers in a constituency committee
room, 1951. Note the cups: 'hot strong
sweet tea, the very taste of English
politics . . .'*

the party. The rest labour, in the main, for their opinions alone. That these may triumph, they take part in an expensive and laborious organisation; spend health and time to little profit and less pleasure . . . and, often at enormous cost both of money and of ease, fight for the cause they love in their own constituencies . . . these offer their help at so much cost to themselves distinctly on the understanding that their own opinions are to prevail . . .'

Thus began the continuing balance, at times marked by tension, between leaders and followers in the Conservative party: the rank and file support the leaders with enthusiasm and hard work – as long as the leaders continue to act in general accord with the wishes of the led.

The major forum for the exposure of those wishes is the Annual Conference, attended by delegates from every local association, by all the officers of the National Union and by the parliamentary party. Resolutions, many hundreds of them, are put forward in advance from local associations all over the country. A committee of the National Union chooses the ones to be debated, usually one or two from each major policy area (foreign affairs, education, defence, etc.). Speakers for and against are called from the floor, and the Conservative Minister (or Shadow Minister) for the subject replies to the debate. A vote is then taken by show of hands unless a ballot is specially requested. But these resolutions passed at Conference are advisory only, not mandatory. The leader of the party (who speaks as the climax at the end) is only required to 'take note' of the party's views and does not take them as instructions.

This is a key difference between the Labour and Conservative parties and is partly a reflection of the fact that the Conservative party is so much older. Its parliamentary power and experience pre-dated mass party organisation by centuries, and the leaders were conscious from the beginning of the dangers implicit in control by an extra-parliamentary unelected 'caucus' of party activists. Hence the stress in speech after speech in the early years of the mass party on the necessity for 'independent judgment' by leaders and MPs, and the advisory consultative role of the rank and file.

Conservative party members, therefore, do not impose policy, but do have the ultimate sanction of withdrawing their support. It was Lord Salisbury, again, during the early years of responsibility to a democratic electorate, who had to lecture his fellow politicians on the danger of pursuing policies the party did not like: 'It is all very well to say that they must vote for you, but they won't work for you and you will find it out at the polls.'

Because Conference resolutions are not mandatory, it is difficult to chart rank and file influence on Conservative policy. (It is easier to chart where they did not have influence: e.g. Conferences from the 1890s to the 1940s had resolutions asking for reform of the House of Lords.) The National Union did, of course, influence events in 1922. It was the threat of a Conference vote against the Liberal–Conservative coalition that forced the parliamentary party to take action in advance. A Conference vote also forced the definite commitment to 'build 300,000 houses' by the 1951 Conservative government. But the influence is rarely so overt and is seen rather in the consistency with which certain themes recur in Conservative policy. The Conservative rank and file, ever since Disraeli delighted thousands of them at the Crystal Palace in 1872 by declaring, 'The Tory Party, unless it is a National Party, is nothing,' have pressed leaders to pursue policies that emphasise patriotism, national unity, personal freedom and a respect for tradition allied to a cautious approach to change. The Conference, symbolically, always closes with massed

Following the 1945 defeat, the party launched a major political education programme for its own membership. Key elements were the Conservative College at Swinton and CPC (Conservative Political Centre) which ran discussion meetings in constituencies and weekend schools. CPC is still active, but Swinton closed in the 1970s.

delegates singing the national anthem. The Labour Conference closes with 'The Red Flag'.

Besides the Conference, there have been from the beginning a plethora of pressure groups and special interest groups inside and outside the party hoping to influence the leadership. In 1911 over a dozen were jostling for position: the Tariff Reform League, the Tariff Commission, Union Defence League, Budget Protest League, Primrose League, Victoria League, Middle Class Defence League, Anti-Socialist Union, Constitutional Speakers League, and at least five other organisations aimed specifically at working men. Someone complained to a Conservative committee on organisation that all these bodies were 'a perfect curse to the party' and 'should be put under some sort of control'.

Special interest groups have been a constant feature of the voluntary party, however, and in the post-war shake-up of the organisation (following the massive defeat of 1945) their existence was positively

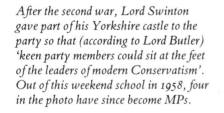

Lord Woolton ('Uncle Fred') was one of the party's best-loved Chairmen. He supervised the post-war organisational overhaul that played an important part in Conservative success in the 1950s. According to one party member Lord Woolton was able to accomplish revolutionary changes because he 'radiated ceaseless benevolence'.

After the second war, Lord Swinton gave part of his Yorkshire castle to the party so that (according to Lord Butler) 'keen party members could sit at the feet of the leaders of modern Conservatism'. Out of this weekend school in 1958, four in the photo have since become MPs.

Hughenden Manor, Buckinghamshire, Disraeli's house.

Primrose League regalia.

Lord Randolph Churchill and the 'Fourth Party'.

The Duke of Rutland, once nearly leader of the party. Vanity Fair cartoon.

Lord Hailsham (Quintin Hogg) rings the 'Victory Bell' at the 1957 annual Conference before presenting it as a gift to the Conference Chairman. The Conference always loves a rousing speaker – as Lord Hailsham swung the bell he shouted 'Let us say to the Labour party: "Send not to ask for whom the bell tolls – it tolls for them!"'

encouraged. The Young Conservatives (YCs), the Conservative Political Centre (CPC, a kind of grass roots 'think tank' where local groups meet monthly to consider policy questions and then send formal reports to the relevant Minister), the Conservative Trade Unionists, Local Government Advisory Group, Federation of Conservative Students, all were initiated by Central Office in the post-war years. Women's Advisory sections of local associations (started when women got the vote) were given fresh encouragement and status. Under Lord Woolton, party chairman in the 1940s, a mass membership drive was launched (based on fund-raising – 'If they've given you money they will feel committed to you') that resulted in a national party membership of well over two million by the early 1950s.

In addition to these special interest groups, there are specialist advisory committees, composed of professionals in the field, who consider individual policy areas and give advice to the leadership on subjects such as education, social services, industry, etc.

All these groups were never designed to work one way only. In addition to collecting rank and file opinion and transmitting it to the leadership, they were (are) expected to act as an 'educative' force and spread the Conservative gospel. Primrose League pamphlet No. 237 published in the 1890s stated its purpose was 'To instruct working men and women how to answer the argument of the Radicals and the Socialists and the Atheists in the workshops and in the public houses and at the street corners . . .'

In the 1920s Conservative agents were being advised that at the 'smoking concerts' in the conservative social clubs they must 'slip in at least one political speech . . .'

In 1935 Miss K. Curlett OBE wrote to *The Imp* (a party magazine) with congratulations on the educational efforts of the West Midlands: 'I read with the greatest interest the Political and Education Programme for the coming autumn drawn up by the West Midlands Federation. This includes a Week-End School, One-Day Schools or evening classes in eleven different centres, fortnightly meetings for Speakers, an Individual Speaking Competition with a section for novices, a Study Group and the organisation of a team of canvassers . . . These all aim at equipping our

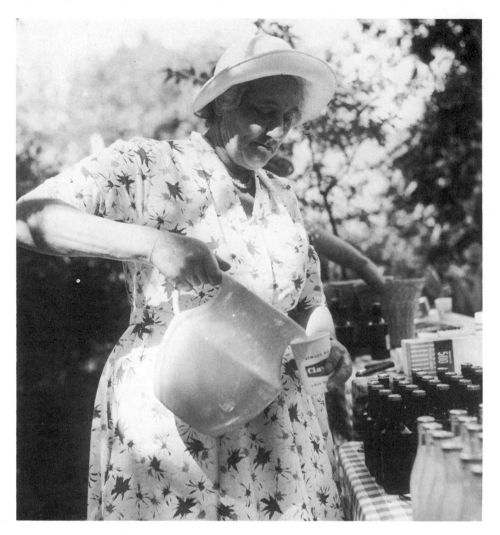

Garden fetes have been a staple of Conservative constituency affairs since the 1880s. Here Dorothy Macmillan, wife of the Prime Minister, does her stint behind the refreshment stand in July 1958.

own members with essential facts – the principles of Conservatism, the application of these principles to present day problems, the method and uses of political organisation.'

It would be a distortion, however, to present the Conservative rank and file solely as activists eager to influence party policy. For a large section of the party, as long as the Conservatives are elected, the most important aspect of the party has always been the social life. And the party managers have been from the beginning highly skilled at presenting to the potential recruit a spicy mix of politics and parties. For years before women even had the vote (or were allowed to sit on party committees) the Primrose League was the most active arm of the voluntary party: organising teas, garden fetes, summer balls, visiting lectures, magic lantern shows . . .

Conference records give one indication of rank and file priorities: there is always an overwhelming demand for tickets and an overpowering crush at the final Leader's Address. In between, the hall during the earnest debates on policy is never full, and the votes on resolutions rarely total the full number of delegates. Coffee bars, lounges, receptions and evening parties are always packed, however, and the whole Conference atmosphere is always more convivial than controversial, more entertaining than educational.

In late Victorian times when the mass party began, managers were not adverse to exploiting the appeal of the aristocracy: National Union stationery was liberally frosted with titles, and tea on the lawns of the manor house was an unfailingly popular lure to party membership. The glittering dinners and balls of the great Edwardian hostesses were lavishly detailed in the popular press and did much to leaven what many saw as the

YC rally in Trafalgar Square, August 1978 From the beginning of the mass organisation in the last century there have always been numerous groups in the party representing special interests. In the organisational shake-up after 1945 their development was positively encouraged.

Garden fete, 1970s version: Prime Minister Edward Heath tips a lady out of bed at the Bexley Conservative Fete.

The distinguishing characteristic of the Conservative rank and file has always been enthusiasm for the leader. Here, YCs demonstrate it at a conference in 1978.

drabness of political debate. At any level it was useful to sweeten the political pill; as the MP for Stoke-on-Trent explained in 1875: 'The object of converting Associations into Clubs is to enable members to obtain recreation as well as knowledge . . . All work and no play makes Jack a dull boy. Merely meeting together to read newspapers has no attraction for many . . . people . . . We have billiard tables and every kind of amusement, together with refreshments . . . The existence of the Club . . . has had a most beneficial effect.'

In every local association from the 1890s to the 1980s, the serious educational programme of the West Midlands Federation would be paralleled by an even longer list of coffee mornings, suppers, theatre trips, strawberry teas, wine and cheese parties, summer festivals, sing-songs, bingo, film shows, cricket matches, barbecues . . . Even if these are nominally fund-raising affairs, the reason people come is because they are social events.

In many rural areas for decades the main focus of community activity was the Primrose League or the Conservative association. In some places this is true even today, while in urban areas where old-style feelings of community do not exist, the socialising role of the party has assumed a new importance.

CHAPTER 4

Roots

IN JANUARY 1830 the political magazine *Quarterly Review* said in an article, 'We are now, as we always have been, decidedly and conscientiously attached to what is called the Tory, and which might with more propriety be called the Conservative Party.' This was (as far as is known) the first time the party was formally called by its modern name. But as the above quotation indicates, the party did not spring suddenly into existence in 1830; indeed, a group called 'Tory' had been a political influence at least as long before as the reign of Charles II.

It is appropriate, however, to date the beginning of the modern party from the 1830s, not only because of the new name, but because the 1832 Reform Act marks such an important divide between the old political world and the new. By effectively removing the last powers of the King to choose ministers, and by beginning to extend – however narrowly at first – the number of people who could vote, the Act created the conditions from which modern political parties emerged.

But the roots from which the Conservative party emerged go a long way back, and it is a favourite amusement of Conservative academics, around firesides on winter evenings, to disagree crudely over the party's genealogy. Can the younger Pitt properly be called a Tory when he called himself a Whig? Does Bolingbroke with his 'Patriot King' deserve a place even though Alexander Pope called him a scoundrel and a coward? Can the Cavaliers with their likable lusty appetite for life be counted in the family tree?

This entertaining, if recondite, disagreement ends, however, when it comes to naming the influences that directly shaped, and the roots that continue to nourish, the modern party. There is remarkable agreement that these were Edmund Burke, Robert Peel and Benjamin Disraeli, whose ideas were subsequently enriched by the Liberal Unionists who joined the party in 1886.

It is interesting and revealing that these three men, most often quoted as the major influences on modern conservatism, were all practising politicians, not academic philosophers. Conservatives have always been suspicious of written doctrines and wary of abstract theories. The importance of these men to the party is not as creators of conservatism – it existed before they did – but as articulators, explainers and practitioners. This is an important point. Conservatism has been around for a long time. Indeed, a case can be made that its basic tenets (a feeling for the past, a cautious approach to change, a preference for order over anarchy) have been part of all human communities. But there are no 'Tory texts' nor written sets of doctrine. 'Many authorities,' says the *Encyclopedia Britannica*, 'consider Conservatism an inarticulate state of mind . . .'

If this is true, it explains the enthusiasm and gratitude which surround the memories of Burke, Peel and Disraeli. They lucidly explained, in words and actions, what many people feel, but find difficult, or impossible, to express.

Edmund Burke was a politically passionate Irishman who came to

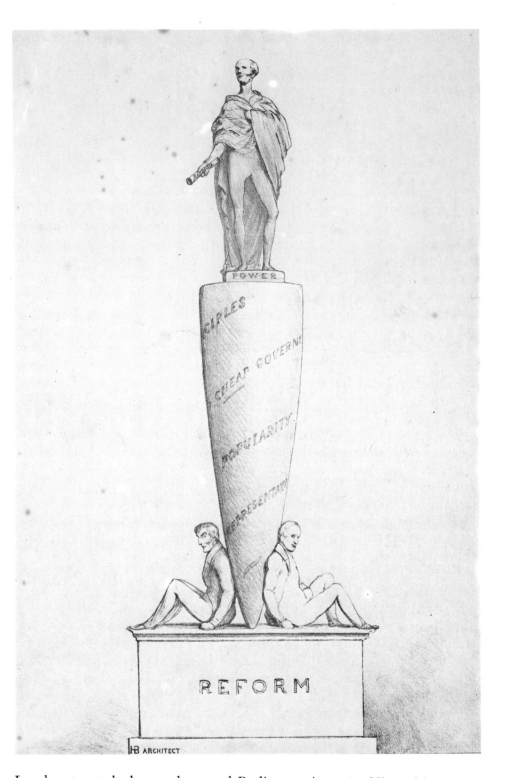

POWER

...CIPLES

CHEAP GOVERN...

POPULARITY

...RESENTAT...

REFORM

HB ARCHITECT

Although a political grouping recognisably 'Tory' had existed in some form for centuries, the reforms of the 1830s marked the proper beginning of the modern party. The Conservatives resisted the reforms at first, but (as the cartoonist here points out) if Wellington and Peel had not supported them in the end, 'the whole superstructure would soon fall to pieces'. 'I see no dignity,' said Peel, 'in persevering in error.'

London to study law and entered Parliament in 1765. His writings are, according to the prime historian of the period, Norman Gash, 'a luminous and profound statement of the fundamental Conservative attitude'.

Sir Robert Peel was a member for 20 years of the Tory governments that preceded the 1832 Reform Act, and after it became the first 'Conservative' Prime Minister.

Disraeli was the dazzling orator whose sharp tongue helped topple Peel – and Peel's party – in 1846, but it was the same eloquence that rebuilt the party and shaped its contemporary form.

All three wrote and spoke to the people of their time, about the particular problems that they faced. It is in a way evidence of the Tory belief in the continuity of human affairs that their words sound so relevant to modern ears.

Burke's most influential work – a bestseller at the time in Britain and abroad – was *Reflections on the Revolution in France*. It was written as a propaganda pamphlet, but its impact is still felt today. Burke was appalled at the Revolutionaries' sweeping destruction of the existing political structure in France and correctly foretold that it would end in anarchy and terror. 'I cannot conceive,' he wrote, 'how any man can have brought himself to that pitch of presumption, to consider his country is nothing but carte blanche upon which he may scribble whatever he pleases.' And further: 'When ancient opinions and rules of life are taken away, the loss cannot possibly be estimated. From that moment we have no compass to govern us; nor can we know distinctly to what port we steer.'

This is a fair description of the Conservative sense of the importance of the past – the necessity to build upon what the past has achieved rather than sweep it all away ('commit waste on the inheritance') and try to begin from scratch. To this respect for the past, however, Burke allied an understanding of the necessity for change: 'A state without the means of some change is without the means of its conservation', and his famous definition of a statesman as one who 'combines a disposition to preserve' with an 'ability to improve'.

Edmund Burke, a seminal and still highly relevant definer of Conservative thought. He saw human society as organic, not mechanistic, and thus counselled change by evolution, not revolution. He warned that 'the greater the power, the greater the abuse'.

The first general election fought on the terms of the 1832 Reform Act decisively influenced the shape of the modern Conservative party: the Conservative and Constitutional Associations (ancestors of constituency associations) were founded to harvest the new votes, and Peel's 'Tamworth Manifesto' to his own constituents (all 586 of them) set a precedent for contemporary party manifestos.

This is the authentic voice of Conservatism, recommending evolution in place of revolution, but pointing out that destruction awaits those who refuse to evolve. It was admirably restated by Peel in his first speech to the reformed House of Commons in 1833. 'I see no dignity,' he said, 'in persevering in error.' And continued that he was 'for reforming every institution that really required reform, but he was for doing it gradually, dispassionately, and deliberately, in order that reform might be lasting.' One of Peel's greatest achievements was not only to reconcile the resentful recalcitrant members of his party to the Reforms of 1832, but also persuade them to support him in even more wide-ranging reforms during his 1841–46 administration.

The Conservative preference for adaptation, not destruction ('change within existing institutions', as Disraeli said) is based on an 'organic' view of society, a feeling that things 'grow', they are not 'made' – that society is, as Burke put it, 'a partnership not only between those who are living, but between those who are living, those who are dead and those who are to be born'. This sense of society as an 'organic whole' implies that men do not simply exist as disparate 'atomistic' elements, but are part of an enduring human community, which both endows them with rights and imposes on them responsibilities.

A second important contribution Burke made to the elucidation of Conservative thought was his insistence that freedom can only exist within the rule of law: 'The only liberty I mean is a liberty connected with order; that not only exists along with order and virtue, but which cannot exist at all without them.' Only inside a framework of laws, which protected the weak from the strong, the minority from the majority, the eccentric from the intolerant, could individuals be free: 'Liberty, too, must be limited in order to be possessed.'

Peel again was the first (perhaps the best) political practitioner of Burke's ideas. His comprehensive reorganisation of the criminal code and creation of the Metropolitan Police reflected Burke's belief that personal freedom is only safe when it 'be ascertained by wise laws, and secured by well constructed institutions'.

Disraeli, also defending the ancient institutions of the land, echoes this theme of ordered freedom: 'The principles of liberty, of order, of law and of religion ought not to be entrusted to individual opinion or to the caprice and passion of multitudes, but should be embodied in a form of permanence and power.'

A third major idea embodied in the speeches and actions of these three men that has had particular relevance for 20th-century Conservatives is the concept that the role of the state in human affairs is limited, but an inescapable part of that role is to (in Disraeli's words) 'elevate the condition of the people'. Peel said in 1837 that he did not want the great machine of government to stand still, he wanted to see it 'animating industry, encouraging production, rewarding toil, correcting what is irregular, purifying what is stagnant or corrupt'. 'Government,' said Burke, 'is a contrivance of human wisdom to provide for human wants. Men have a right that these wants should be provided for by this wisdom.' He went on: 'Whatever each man can separately do, without trespassing upon others, he has a right to do for himself; and he has a right to a fair portion of all which society, with all its combinations of skill and force, can do in his favour.'

It was to these basic themes of Conservativism that the Liberal Unionists in 1886 added their passionate and invigorating belief in individual freedom and the limitless possibilities of human achievement. Most had been followers of Gladstone (who was himself a protégé of Peel and had been a junior treasury minister in Peel's first administration), but Gladstone's stand on Irish Home Rule sent a sizeable number of them into the Tory camp, where they remained and were formally merged in 1912. The full name of the party today commemorates this alliance: it is properly titled 'The Conservative and Unionist Party'.

Liberalism, too, was an inarticulate creed before a political one, born from the experience of self-made men who seized the opportunities the times offered and who created, often from nothing, flourishing empires of commerce and industry. They were convinced by their own experience that equality of opportunity and personal freedom were the most important things in life. 'The sole end,' said John Stuart Mill, the Liberals' most lucid prophet, 'for which mankind are warranted, individually or collectively, in interfering with the liberty of action of any of their number, is self-protection.' And 'The only freedom which deserves the name is that of pursuing our own good in our own way, so long as we do not attempt to deprive others of theirs, or impede their efforts to obtain it.' Mill added a warning: 'A state which dwarfs its men, in order that they may be more docile instruments in its hands even for beneficial purposes – will find that with small men nothing great can be accomplished.'

The Liberal ideas accorded well with much traditional Conservative thought (indeed, much Liberal thinking could be traced to Burke and Peel as well), and by the 1890s the Conservative Prime Minister, Lord Salisbury, was saying, 'The protection of each individual human being from more interference than is indispensably necessary to protect the freedom of his neighbours, is what we used to understand as the meaning of freedom.'

Although it is possible to identify all these influences on Conservative thought, it would be wrong to imply that there exists a coherent body of

Robert Peel: as party leader and then Prime Minister in the formative years of modern Parliamentary democracy, his actions as much as his words moulded the modern Tory party. Among his oft-quoted injunctions: 'Of all the vulgar arts of government, that of solving every difficulty which might arise by thrusting the hand into the public purse is the most delusory and contemptible.' National Portrait Gallery, London.

dogma to which Conservatives refer. The *Encyclopedia Britannica*, again, points out, 'Conservatism is less a creed than a cause, and less a political philosophy than a political tradition.'

Conservative politicians have always leaned toward pragmatism rather than any more formal 'ism'. 'What is the use,' said Burke, 'of discussing a man's abstract right to food or medicine? The question is upon the method of procuring and administering them.' And Disraeli pointed out with practical candour that not political abstractions, but 'increased means and increased leisure are the two civilizers of man.'

And Conservatives at large do not, in the words of Lord Hailsham, 'believe that political struggle is the most important thing in life . . . To the great majority of Conservatives, religion, art, study, family, country, friends, music, fun, duty, all the joy and riches of existence of which the poor no less than the rich are the indefeasible freeholders, all these are higher in the scale than their handmaiden, the political struggle.'

CHAPTER 5

Winning and Losing

IN THE 19th century the major requirement for political campaigning was money. In the 20th it is stamina.

In 1832 the Reform Act enlarged the electorate, made parliamentary representation more equable and took a stab at controlling some of the more blatant corruption. However, to the discouragement of idealists, many of the new electorate did not view their vote as a tool of political power, but gleefully regarded it as a financial asset, and sold it to the highest bidder. In an ordinary election (even an uncontested one) in the 1830s–1850s, a single vote could bring £1, and a 'plumper' fetched £2 (in a two-member constituency each elector had two votes and could 'plump' them both for one candidate). In a hot contest a vote withheld till near the end of polling might command £30 or more.

Buying votes, of course, was illegal, but even without overt bribery a candidate was personally responsible for election expenses which could run to thousands of pounds. Greville said Lord Douro and Scarlett spent £50,000 to be elected at Norwich in 1837, which was extravagant; but then Mary Ann Disraeli told Peel that in Disraeli's Maidstone election 'more than £40,000 was spent through my influence only'. A candidate had to pay for the polling booths, the salaries of officials, the expenses of administering the oaths, the transport of electors to and from the polls, and anything else that might conceivably be termed an election expense.

John Gorst, Disraeli's Principal Agent at Central Office (who had been living with this system intimately for years) described what it was like: 'the practice had become almost universal for candidates to lavish immense sums of money upon purposes not in themselves corrupt, but quite useless for the attainment of any legitimate object. The true object of such expenditure was to distribute money amongst the greatest possible number of electors, and a candidate who refused to conform to this universal custom had, or was believed to have, no chance of being returned . . . Every article purchased, every service rendered, was paid for at more than double its market value . . . To insure that everybody should be aware of the existence of the candidate it was usual to have his name posted in gigantic characters all over the neighbourhood, thus affording lucrative employment to printers and bill-stickers, and an excuse for payments to the owners of premises on which the posters were displayed. Each side was accustomed to engage in a merry warfare by posting their own bills over those of their opponents, thus causing the initial expenditure to be repeated again and again, and giving occasion to a fresh employment of electors as watchmen to prevent the bills being torn down . . . Both sides concurred in a complete distrust of the post-office, and employed an army of messengers to deliver their communications to the electors, with not half the certainty but with ten times the expense. Canvassers were engaged to go round and ask the electors how they intended to vote, in some cases in such excessive numbers that they could find nothing to do but meet in public houses and canvass one another . . .'

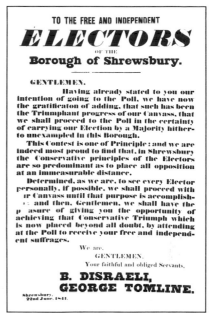

TO THE FREE AND INDEPENDENT
ELECTORS
OF THE
Borough of Shrewsbury.

GENTLEMEN.
Having already stated to you our intention of going to the Poll, we have now the gratification of adding, that such has been the Triumphant progress of our Canvass, that we shall proceed to the Poll in the certainty of carrying our Election by a Majority hither-to unexampled in this Borough.

This Contest is one of Principle; and we are indeed most proud to find that, in Shrewsbury the Conservative principles of the Electors are so predominant as to place all opposition at an immeasurable distance.

Determined, as we are, to see every Elector personally, if possible, we shall proceed with ir Canvass until that purpose is accomplish- and then, Gentlemen, we shall have the p asure of giving you the opportunity of achieving that Conservative Triumph which is now placed beyond all doubt, by attending at the Poll to receive your free and independent suffrages.

We are,
GENTLEMEN,
Your faithful and obliged Servants,
B. DISRAELI,
GEORGE TOMLINE.
Shrewsbury,
22nd June, 1841.

Disraeli's election notice for Shrewsbury, 1841. It was his sixth election campaign in nine years – he only won two of them. He won this one despite his opponent's broadcasting his considerable debts. Mrs Disraeli campaigned furiously on his behalf – 'Such a gay lady, Sir!' his constituents told him.

Westminster election 1863, the nomination in Covent Garden. Each elector had two votes and could 'plump' them both for one candidate. Hence the two man Grosvenor–Mill ticket urged 'No plumping'. Rain continues to be a feature of British elections.

Bringing electors to the polls, November 1868. Everyone basked in the candidate's largesse: 'on the day of polling there was a grand field-day of all the cabdrivers, messengers, canvassers, clerks, agents and watchers employed in bringing the independent electors to the poll, all entitled not only to special pay . . . but to reasonable refreshment . . .'

Lord Salisbury (on steps, left) visits Ulster, 1898. Before radio and television, political celebrities attracted crowds of thousands. Their speeches (sometimes lasting hours) were intently listened to and earnestly discussed.

Elections, not surprisingly, were viewed with great enthusiasm by nearly everyone except the candidate. It was not only that cash and treats rained down upon voters and non-voters alike; the entire spectacle could be highly entertaining, with bands, parades, buntings, fights between rival gangs of supporters, and a marked lack of respect toward candidates compared to our day. Lady Charlotte Guest records that at the elections in Poole in 1850 the mob pelted the candidates first with rotten eggs, apples and turnips, then flour, which stuck, she said, 'where the eggs had already taken effect and giving all the party on the hustings the appearance of being so many millers'.

The climax of the campaigns were two full days for polling during which electors presented themselves in public to the returning officer and announced out loud their choice. This system did have the merit for candidates who had bought votes of confirming they got their money's worth (after secret ballots came in in 1872 complaints were heard that some electors were accepting bribes from both sides), but it was hard to pretend intimidation did not exist, especially when landlords were running and tenants were voting.

For most of the 19th century each candidate ran his own campaign as best he could – or could afford. National co-ordination was very weak, although *The Times* did print speeches by the party leaders and, by printing Peel's 'Tamworth Manifesto' to his own electors, set a very early precedent for the national party manifestos of the next century.

Then in the 1870s and 1880s four events coincided to cause a profound change in the nature of political campaigning: the beginnings of a mass electorate, the founding of national party organisations, the effective control of electoral corruption and widespread adult literacy. To this was

A woman arrives to vote, 1919. Votes for women transformed campaigning as had votes for workers in 1867. Candidates had to appeal to an enlarged electorate with different concerns, and the effect can be seen in the campaign literature.

Baldwin poses for a publicity picture. He was the first politician to master the new techniques of 20th-century campaigning. Over the radio he chatted, others orated. He also prepared with care: in the 1929 campaign he wrote to the BBC asking about the social composition of the likely audience and whether working men listened at home or in pubs.

Nancy Astor campaigning in 1919 when women voters were a novelty, let alone a woman candidate.

Techniques change, rituals remain. All elections begin with the Monarch dissolving Parliament and calling a new one to attend. Here the George VI Proclamation of 3rd February 1950 is posted outside Mansion House after the ceremonial reading by the City of London Common Crier.

added, in the 1890s, the cheap popular press, and the conditions that were to shape 20th-century campaigning were set.

A mass electorate (constituencies number now between 60,000 and 70,000 voters) cannot be appealed to by individual canvass. They cannot be appealed to in any of the ways outlawed by the Corrupt Practices Act of 1883 (bribery, 'treating', or undue influence – i.e. violence). They must therefore be persuaded, either by propaganda put out by the party, or by publicity (speeches, etc.) reported in the press, radio and television. (As early as 1875 a prescient speaker at the party Conference was exhorting his colleagues to 'look to' the local press: 'The most powerful of all influences is the Press, and no Association should be content unless it has in close connection with it some local organ of public opinion.')

Since the Corrupt Practices Act severely limited the amount of money any single candidate could spend, propaganda and publicity had to be done for the party as a whole by the national organisation. (Back in 1876 the National Union announced proudly that they had 'printed upwards of 700,000 pamphlets, about 600,000 of which have been distributed gratuitously'.)

Centralised publicity efforts meant that national themes had to be agreed upon, as all candidates would have to campaign under the same propaganda umbrella. For the Conservatives, the general themes they were to fight under had already been laid down by Disraeli before his great victory in 1874: a simple but remarkably effective combination of patriotism, national unity and social reform ('the elevation of the condition of the people'). Their efficacy is best judged against electoral performance; in the 100 years after Disraeli became Prime Minister (1874–1974), the Conservatives were in power alone, or in a Conservative-dominated coalition, for 67 years, more than twice as long as any other single party.

The electoral reforms of the late 19th and early 20th centuries meant that propaganda and publicity became functions of the national organisation. But individual candidates still had to fight and win individual constituencies, so that Parliamentary campaigns in this century have become oddly split between the national campaigns, conducted with the ever more powerful and glamorous organs of the electronic media, and the individual constituency campaigns, which continue to be conducted in much the same way as they were over fifty years ago.

Harold Macmillan wrote of his early campaigns in the 1920s and 1930s: 'I remember very well, once an election had started, feeling as if a great shutter had come down between us and the rest of the world. There we were, isolated in Stockton, working away day after day, night after night, in what seemed a sort of fog. (One had something of the same experience in a great battle, like Loos or the Somme.) . . . In each constituency separate engagements were being waged without much regard for the main armies. Generally, we held three or four meetings a night in small schoolrooms . . . for some reason the school official, either because he was a Socialist or from a perverted sense of humour, generally only made available the infants' school, where the seating was ill-suited to the ample forms of the audience. In addition to a few afternoon meetings and some women's meetings, there was the perpetual canvassing, through one street after another . . .'

In the 1950s, the wife of a Conservative MP, veteran of three campaigns, gave an even more personal view of a local campaign: 'The wife's part in this process is almost entirely physical – slogging always (or so it seems) through wind, sleet, snow and rain, by day and by night, on pavements or across muddy fields, or up endless flights of stairs in blocks

Early morning at the West Acton polling station, 23rd February 1950. The 'tellers' – one from each party – check who has voted so that at the end of the day they can fetch forgetful supporters to do their duty.

Cars speeded campaigning up, but all
politicians still took their message to the
streets.

Eve-of-poll speech, 24th October 1951,
by the one 20th-century campaigner
guaranteed to draw a mass audience.
Churchill was then 77 and about to
become Prime Minister again.

Churchill in the Cabinet Room at Downing St. on VE Day, 1945.

Churchill, Roosevelt and Stalin at the Yalta Conference, February 1945.

Churchill's studio in his country house, Chartwell, Kent.

The dining-room at Chartwell.

of flats, while her soles grow paper-thin and her hair more and more bedraggled . . . she makes quick visits to crowded committee rooms, and, standing still coated . . . drinks at each a large, hot, strong, sweet cup of tea, the very taste of English politics, among the trestle-tables stacked with papers and posters, overlaid with huge sheets of brown paper backing electoral lists defaced with red and blue, and weighted here and there with the big brown tea-pot; the large square biscuit tin . . . and the plate for the tea-money.'

The insular nature of local campaigns had not changed much in 1964, when the Nuffield College study of the election by David Butler and Anthony King recorded: 'If candidates and agents were surprisingly unaware of what was going on at the national level, party workers were still more so, while total indifference seemed to characterise most of the electorate.'

Yet increasingly, academic studies of modern elections insist that local campaigns, no matter how energetically waged, have less and less influence on the ultimate result. Voters are far more influenced, according to the experts, by the party's national image and the leader's performance as exhibited in the press and on television.

This puts an enormous burden on the leader and the small group who determine national propaganda themes. If they get it wrong ('it' = the mood of the electorate), they can wreck not only their own careers, but the fortunes of the entire party (and, partisans would say, the fortunes of the country too). There was a kind of murky period between the coming of mass voting and the arrival of reliable opinion polls when divining 'it' was a very tricky business. Balfour certainly got it wrong in 1906, and not only led the party to smashing defeat, but even lost his own seat. In 1929 and 1945 the party again badly misjudged the public mood and suffered for it at the polls. But in the years 1951 to 1959 the party won three general elections in a row, increasing their majority each time. This unprecedented record was capped by Macmillan's triumphant 1959 campaign under the slogan 'Life's better with the Conservatives'.

Then from 1964 to 1974 the Conservatives lost four elections and won one. But the actual results in this period are confusing for party strategists: no party won an overall majority in any contest, and the popular votes (as

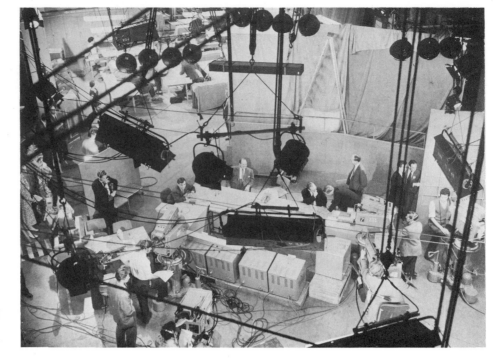

BBC-TV prepares for election night, 1959. By the 1960s television was established as the dominant medium for political publicity, and the channels vied with each other for the most dramatic polling night coverage.

Ernest Marples, a vigorous campaigner as candidate and Minister of Transport, climbs up to hear a voter's views.

compared to seats in Parliament) were dramatically close: in 1964 Labour won 44.1% of the vote, the Conservatives 43.4%. In 1970 it was Conservatives 46.4%, Labour 43.0%; in February 1974, Labour 37.2%, Conservatives 38.2%.

Then in May 1979 the Conservatives won with a clear 7% margin over Labour, representing a national swing of 5.2%, and resulting in a Parliamentary majority of 44 over all opposition parties combined.

The 1979 Tory campaign differed from previous ones in its sharply detailed platform – 'too explicit', warned many observers in advance of the election. It also differed in its use of the highly professional advertising agency Saatchi & Saatchi, whose sophisticated hard-hitting ads ('Labour Isn't Working', '1984 – What would Britain be like after another 5 years of Labour Government?') contrasted sharply with the more genteel slogans of the 1950s and 1960s.

Before, and especially during, a contemporary election campaign, experts in many fields are employed at the national level of the party: sifting the public opinion surveys, analysing by-election results, preparing detailed, extremely comprehensive background material for candidates (the *Campaign Guide* now runs to nearly 800 pages), organising press briefings, television interviews and national tours for the leader, and producing advertising material for national distribution. All of which contrasts oddly with the trestle tables and the tea-pots that remain the basic tools of the local campaign.

The proof of all the efforts, national and local, comes on polling day – and a very sober affair that is now, compared to the 1800s. All campaigning activity at national headquarters ceases, and the action shifts to the rooms with the trestle tables. In theory Conservative canvassers

Richard Price, Conservative candidate in Paddington North, listens to a constituent in 1969. Politicians today are personally far more accessible to their electors than their 19th-century counterparts.

Trafalgar Square election night, 18th June 1970. This was the first election in which 18-year-olds could vote, the last step towards full adult suffrage, a process begun in 1832. Pollsters, relying in part on the presumed views of the new young voters, predicted a Conservative defeat. In fact the Tories won with a majority of 30 seats.

Politicians, party workers, journalists and voters all expected an election in October 1978. When it failed to happen, Conservatives responded with ads like this. The poster campaign (another one was 'Labour isn't working' featuring a long dole queue) continued through the winter.

will have identified all the Conservative voters in a constituency; Conservative 'tellers' at every polling booth will check them off as they vote. Toward the end of the day, if the system is working, the volunteers in the committee rooms will be able to tell which supporters have yet to do their duty and send 'knockers-up' to remind them. This activity, of course, can influence a result only in a marginal contest, not in one where thousands of votes separate the parties.

Candidates themselves are superfluous to the party organisation on polling day and are usually sent to tour the polling booths, modestly thanking officials and volunteers for their efforts. It is all a far cry from the election days of John Gorst: 'Finally on the day of polling there was a grand field-day of all the cabdrivers, messengers, canvassers, clerks, agents and watchers employed in bringing the independent electors to the poll, all entitled not only to special pay by reason of the arduous and peculiar character of their services, but to "reasonable refreshment" supplied to them with unstinted liberality by the publicans of their party.'

CHEER UP! LABOUR CAN'T HANG ON FOR EVER.

THE CONSERVATIVE PARTY

CHAPTER 6
The Machine

THE LEGEND of the power of the 'Tory machine' brings comfort to the faithful and helps demoralise the opposition ('Compared with our opponents we [Labour] are still at the penny-farthing stage in a jet propelled era,' wailed the Harold Wilson Report on Party Organisation in 1955); so it is no wonder it is fostered in Conservative literature.

Inside the party itself the organisation has actually been more often blamed for defeat than credited with victory. Indeed, every major electoral loss has sparked off a complete overhaul of the party machinery. Lord Blake, in his book on the Conservative party, says this is because in defeat everyone is cross and has time on their hands. Certainly every serious rebuff at the polls – 1880, 1906, 1929, 1945 and 1964 – has been followed by a vigorous shake-up of the organisation.

Interestingly, although these shake-ups have occasioned much activity and re-shuffling of people and titles, the basic Conservative organisation remains the same now as when Disraeli and John Gorst set it up following the 1867 electoral reforms. Then – as now – the organisation (it has been called a 'machine' ever since Lord Hampton said the splendid victory of 1874 was in part due to 'the working of this great machine') had three parts: the Parliamentary party (the MPs), the National Union (composed of all the affiliated but autonomous local associations) and Central Office (the paid professionals, a kind of civil service who act as secretariat, liaison, research and publicity agency for the other two parts). All three are ultimately responsible to the leader of the party, who appoints the ministers who head the Parliamentary party, and the Chairman and Vice Chairmen who head Central Office. The National Union, however, elects its own officers.

Over the years the size, techniques and personnel may have changed, but this basic structure has not, nor has its purpose, which has always been crystal clear: to get Conservative candidates elected to office.

'We have recognised,' said the Maxwell-Fyfe Committee charged with re-organising the party after 1945, 'the need not so much for a constitution which seems tidy to the student of political history or logical in all respects, as for an organisation which is an educative political force and a machine for winning elections.'

Although Disraeli and John Gorst set up the formal structure of the organisation in response to the 1867 electoral reforms, its roots really go back to Peel and his response to the 1832 reforms. In both cases a new electoral situation had been created, and the party needed to adapt itself if it wanted its candidates to win.

A key feature of the 1832 Act, fastened on by Peel although little noticed by others, was the requirement to set up a register in every constituency of men able to vote. The responsibility to register, however, rested with the voter, and he had to pay (one shilling) for the privilege. This did not change until the 1918 Act, which gave the vote to women, also gave the responsibility for registering voters to the state. In the 19th century many would not have bothered to register but for the urgings

Mr Isaac Lyons, a local Conservative Agent in the 1890s. The burden of ensuring the Corrupt Practices Act was not infringed fell wholly upon the Agent (it still does), who fought many battles in the election courts. Agents were also responsible until 1918 for seeing voters were registered.

Chairman's Copy.

THE NATIONAL UNION OF CONSERVATIVE & CONSTITUTIONAL ASSOCIATIONS

RULES

Passed at a CONFERENCE, held on NOVEMBER 12th 1867.

I.—The name of the Society shall be the National Union of Conservative and Constitutional Associations, and its object to constitute a centre for such bodies.

II.—Every such Association, subscribing One Guinea or more per annum to the funds, may, by vote of the Council, be admitted a Member of the Union, *but the Council shall have the power to place on the Register of the Union gratuitously, the names of any Conservative or Constitutional Associations which may desire it.*

III.—Any Branch or Affiliated Association consisting of not less than 100 Members, may, either in common with its Chief or Parent Association, or alone, be admitted, on a separate subscription as an individual Member of the Union.

IV.—Each Association shall be entitled to send two Representatives to attend and vote at any conference of the Union.

Minutes of Proceedings at the First Conference of the National Union of Conservative & Constitutional Associations held at the Freemasons' Tavern Novr 12. 1867.

Mr Gorst, M.P. for Cambridge in the Chair.

The following towns sent delegates to the Conference: Bacup, Bath, Birmingham and six branches, Blackburn, Bolton, Bristol, Carlisle, Canterbury, Chatham, Colchester, Crewe, Charlton, Croydon, Deptford, Devonport, Dover, Eccles, Falmouth, Gravesend, Greenwich, Guildford, Hull, Harwich, Halifax, Hertford, Hereford, Hastings, Cdle, Ipswich, Kidderminster, King's Lynn, Lambeth, London and Westminster and four branches, Liverpool, Manchester, Maidstone, Norwich, Newcastle, Peckham, Penryn, Portsmouth, Reading, Rochester, Rotherhithe, Shipley.

Above left The National Union was created in response to the 1867 Reform Act in hopes of influencing the new voters. It was to be the national body representing local Constitutional and Conservative Working Men's Associations which already existed.

Above right Handwritten minutes of the first National Union meeting in November 1867. John Gorst, in the Chair, was MP for Cambridge City then, but lost his seat in the 1868 election. He then became Principal Agent, and his influence on the shape of the party is still apparent.

(persuasive and monetary) of the candidate and his agent. 'Register! Register! Register!' cried Peel to his Tamworth electors in 1841. 'The battle of the Constitution will be fought in the Registration Courts!'

Due in part to the work of Peel and his indefatigable helper Francis Robert Bonham (sometime MP and full-time party manager) Conservative Registration Societies were started all over the country. These societies evolved in some cases into the local Conservative Associations which affiliated to the National Union and went on to become the grass-roots base of the 20th-century national organisation.

These local associations have always been in principle wholly autonomous: they raise their own funds, pay their own expenses, choose their own candidates and run their own campaigns.

In practice, of course, they are supported in all these activities by the national headquarters, the Central Office. Central Office, officially set up in 1870, had its roots in the work of Peel and Bonham as well. Operating out of the Carlton Club in St James's Street (founded in 1832 specifically as a Conservative political-cum-social club), Peel and Bonham together fostered the development of the local registration societies, dealt with national publicity and co-ordinated the business of finding candidates for seats and seats for candidates. So successful were they, that in 1841, a bare six years after the party had been written off as wrecked by the battles over the Reform Act, it managed to field nearly 500 candidates, and to win a majority of 76 in the House of Commons. It was agreed by all to be a victory of superior organisation, and thus began the legend of the invincible Tory machine.

69 St James's St., formerly Arthur's Club, now the home of the Carlton, the most famous political club of all, where so much Tory drama and intrigue has taken place. Peel and Bonham virtually ran the party from the Carlton in the 1830s and 1840s, and it was the scene of the famous 1922 meeting that withdrew support from Lloyd George. The Carlton moved here after their Pall Mall premises were bombed in 1940.

32 Smith Square, Conservative Central Office and headquarters of the National Union.

Richard Middleton, the supreme party agent. With Lord Salisbury he created the Conservative 'machine', the outlines of which remain today. In gratitude the party presented him with £10,000 and a silver casket containing the names of 4000 of the faithful who contributed, engrossed on vellum.

It was given a further boost by two subsequent and equally felicitous partnerships between gifted politicians and superb party managers: Disraeli with John Gorst and Lord Salisbury with Richard Middleton.

Disraeli knew from the first that the electoral reforms of 1867 called for a whole new approach to party organisation. Looking around, it was said, for 'a young and ambitious Conservative who would be ready to devote the best years of his life to working out a scheme', he lit upon John Gorst and made him Principal Agent. As Gorst himself had said in chairing the first meeting of the National Union in 1867, the purpose of the new organisation was not 'for discussion of Conservative principles on which we are all agreed', but rather to discover 'by what particular organisation we may make these Conservative principles effective among the masses'. In other words, to win elections.

The 'particular organisation' devised by Gorst and refined by his successor Richard Middleton had three basic functions: to provide a steady supply of candidates with reasonable credentials; to do national publicity and propaganda; and to offer efficient support to local associations. Just about the same things that Peel and Bonham were doing from the Carlton Club. To these three functions was added, in 1929, the job of doing research to aid policy formation.

The key to efficient support for local associations in the 19th century, and today, is the paid professional agent. This position in the Conservative party evolved from the personal agents that used to be employed by each candidate. The task of the candidate's agent before 1918 was to get supporters on to the register and into the polling booth, and then afterwards to defend their right to vote against the opponent's inevitable

Inside Conservative headquarters, 1950. The 1945 defeat caused a major shake-up in the party. Under R.A. Butler the Research Department launched a huge education/propaganda campaign aimed at modernising the party's thinking as well as influencing the electorate.

Left *The propaganda umbrella under which all Conservative candidates campaign is determined at national level. Central Office provides the constituencies with leaflets, posters, digests of facts. This collection is for the 1950 campaign.*

Opposite page below *The annual Agents Conference, November 1894. The night before this photo was taken, the Agents had consumed the following dinner washed down with eight different wines:*

Soups
Clear Oxtail Puree Portugaise
Fish
Boiled Turbot Hollandaise Sauce
Fried Fillets Sole Tartar Sauce
Entrees
Compote of Pigeon
Ballotine of Veal à la Toulouse
Joints
Sirloin Beef Saddle Mutton
Boiled Turkey and Celery Sauce
York Ham
Sweets
Victoria Pudding Meringues
Apricot Tartlets Wine Jellies
Stewed fruit and Custard
Dessert
Coffee Liqueurs

The Mobile Bookshop in Bexleyheath, 1948, signing up supporters two years in advance of the next election. The legendary Tory 'machine' is based on superior recruitment and organisation of volunteers.

challenges. If his own candidate lost the agent challenged the victor's voters. The challenges were often to good effect as dead men, paupers and even complete figments were often discovered on the rolls. 'I do not see how we can win,' whispered Mr Rigby's agent (in Disraeli's novel *Coningsby*), 'we have polled all our dead men, and Millbank is seven ahead.'

The Corrupt Practices Act of 1883 increased the importance of the election agent, as it became his responsibility (on pain of prosecution) to see the provisions of the act were not infringed. A fortuitous side effect was that by limiting the amount of money the party could spend on other things (e.g. bribing voters) the Act released resources that went to pay for more and better agents. Throughout the 1890s the special magazine published for Conservative agents, *The Tory*, was full of advice on how to catch the opposition in corrupt practices (and so void the result if they won) and of reports of protracted battles in the courts following each election. The clean and quiet British elections of the late 20th century (their purity is a continual source of astonishment to foreign visitors) is due not only to the Corrupt Practices Act itself, but to the strenuous efforts (albeit in their own interests) by election agents to see it is enforced.

A second function of the national organisation has always been publicity and propaganda. In the first seven years of its existence it produced and distributed 500,000 pamphlets and 300,000 circulars, and by 1929 the publishing efforts had reached a fever pitch: 85,159,776 leaflets and pamphlets were distributed in that year – enough for every man, woman and child in the country to have two. Unfortunately the Conservatives lost the 1929 election. Today the organisation's emphasis has shifted from publishing vast quantities of its own material to concentration on press releases to the mass media and on straightforward advertising. They do publish a monthly newsletter (circulation 200,000), the Conservative Manifesto at election time and specialist booklets on aspects of policy.

A third, and crucial, function of the national organisation remains the maintenance of a list of Parliamentary candidates for Westminster and Europe from which constituency associations can choose. Hundreds of applications to be a Conservative candidate are received every year at Central Office. A selection committee, headed by one of the party's vice-chairmen (usually an MP) and composed of a representative group of party members, sifts the applications and compiles the list. Their criteria are not divulged.

Having compiled the list, and presented it to constituencies that request it, the power of the national organisation ends. There is an irrepressible myth – not true – that Central Office instructs constituencies whom to choose as candidates. Perhaps they would like to, but in fact utter autonomy in candidate selection is the most jealously guarded prerogative of a local association. Even advice as to type is firmly refused: Sir George Younger, chairman of the party in the 1920s, when the new women's vote was being wooed, said despairingly: 'I have tried my very best to get constituencies to accept a lady candidate, and one chairman wrote back saying I had given him the shock of his life.'

The only contemporary function of the national organisation not anticipated by Peel, Bonham, Disraeli and Gorst is the Research Department. (Given their views on the limited role of government they would have been appalled at the gigantic extension of government activity that has made the Research Department necessary.) It was formed in 1929 by Baldwin and Neville Chamberlain, and from the beginning has had a key

The election results board. Many local Conservative associations have benefited from the war experience of their Agent or Chairman, and campaigns are often run with military efficiency.

Party worker at Central Office prepares parcels of election literature for candidates in the 1955 election. Producing literature has been a major activity of the party headquarters since the 1870s and 1880s when the National Union spent nearly two-thirds of its annual budget on literature and lecturers.

The National Union is the main vehicle for Conservative fund-raising. Here the Chancellor of the Exchequer Heathcoat Amory and other members of the platform party encourage the delegates to the 1958 Conference to contribute.

role. 'Through my new department,' said Chamberlain with satisfaction when he became its head, 'I shall have my finger on the springs of policy.'

Under 'Rab' (later Lord) Butler in the 1945–51 period the department was particularly influential in reconciling the party to postwar realities. The party could no longer 'sit in entrenched positions or rely on holding old-fashioned fortresses,' said Butler, and he spearheaded an educational and propaganda effort that undoubtedly influenced the Conservative victory in 1951, and also laid the foundations for the reformist legislation of the 1950s.

The Research Department has grown in contemporary times to a position of immense importance. It continuously commissions and analyses public opinion surveys, produces in-depth policy studies, prepares every week a pithy backgrounding to current issues that circulates to all MPs and key party officials; it produces the *Campaign Guide*, giving information and statistics on every current topic from abortion to youth service. The Research Department is also intimately involved in preparing the party election manifesto.

Of course when most people think of the 'Tory machine', they are in fact thinking not of the Central Office, but of a local association. 'Witnessed a singular spectacle on my way home this evening,' wrote Laurence Marks as 'Pooter' in *The Observer* during the 1976 Carshalton by-election. 'As I turned the corner out of Station Approach, I beheld our Conservative opponent, Nigel Forman, sprinting along the street, pursued by a galloping horde of young ladies carrying leaflets. Gowing told me that Tories always campaign at the double, which alarms newspaper reporters and other persons of a nervous disposition who fear being trampled to death.'

There is some truth in the image of an overpowering Tory machine at local level. Especially in associations where retired army officers become Chairman or Agent, campaigns can be run with military panache: ward rooms with giant campaign maps marked off with coloured pins, printed daily schedules, squads of canvassers reporting in and being briefed by the duty officer, a special aide de camp who stays with the candidate at all times . . . In a marginal seat (and elections these days are won and lost in the marginals) this kind of organisation can make the difference. The Conservatives did – for example – win the Carshalton by-election.

CHAPTER 7

Frictions, Factions and Splits

ONE OF the most striking things about the life of the Conservative party is the oft-repeated announcement of its death.

Regularly every generation since 1830, when the *Quarterly Review* christened Peel's coalition 'The Conservatives', the party's obituary has been written. At the very first, in 1832, the diminished ranks and demoralised state of the Parliamentary party led Lord Mahon to write to Peel in despair: 'We as a party are suspended', and 'from our weakness we must be umpires rather than parties in the great struggle which the new House is so shortly to witness.' Then in 1846 the Corn Law schisms appeared to have dealt the party a mortal blow – it was twenty years before they returned to power. They were barely there when the 1867 Reform Act caused Lord Derby to gloomily predict: 'This is the end of the Conservative Party', a prediction exultantly endorsed by Karl Marx, then resident in London, who saw it as the 'inevitable result' of universal suffrage.

In the 20th century after virtually every election defeat, the pessimistic have been ready with black crepe, and yet each time the party has rallied, regrouped and won at the polls again.

These recurring rejuvenative powers have been rivalled only by the party's digestive powers. In its century and a half of life it has absorbed, transcended or managed to ignore a remarkable collection of factions, splinter groups, ginger groups, sects and cabals – from Disraeli's outrageously romantic 'Young England' to Joe Chamberlain's radical Liberals; from Randolph Churchill's 'Tory Democracy' to the 'United Empire Party' of Lords Beaverbrook and Rothermere. This absorptive ability has been commented on by two leading contemporary Tories: 'It is because we are an *inclusive* party,' said Norman St John Stevas, 'not an *exclusive* one.' And because, according to Ian Gilmour, 'The Tory aim is harmony, not unison.'

People who live peacefully outside politics among friends with whom they agree tend to forget that human society is full of disagreement, and politics only exist as proxy for the pistol or the club. It is a necessary condition that any live political body be full of disagreement, dispute and dissent. 'Party divisions,' said Burke, 'whether on the whole operating for good or evil, are things inseparable from free goverment.' This is as true intra-party as inter-party. The surprising thing is not that frictions, factions and splits have accompanied the whole history of the party, but that they have been so successfully contained, and that the Conservatives have continued to exist as a recognisable entity for 150 years.

The 19th century in particular was a testing time for political stability: during those years Britain changed from a country with a population of 12 million to one of over 40 million; from a nation where half the population lived on farms to one where 80% lived in towns and cities; from one where a limited aristocratic oligarchy ruled supreme to one with a democratic government elected on something approaching universal suffrage.

Peel introducing the repeal of the Corn Laws to the Commons, 1846. Peel had decided the tax on grain was intolerable, but the Tory agriculturists were outraged by his action; the party split outright between protectionists and free traders and did not regain real power for nearly 30 years.

The commotion over the 1867 Reform Act followed by the Conservative defeat in 1868 made a section of the party very anxious to replace Derby with Salisbury as leader of the Lords and thus displace Disraeli as leader of the Commons. They did not succeed.

THE RIVAL KINGS: OR, WHO SHALL LEAD THE LORDS?

THE TROUBLESOME TRIO

APPEARING NIGHTLY DURING THE PERFORMANCE OF "IMPATIENCE" AT ST. STEPHEN'S.

L(rd R-ND-LPH CH-RCH-LL, Sir DR-MM-ND W-LFF, and Mr. ASHM-D B-RTL-TT, ensemble—

WE'VE long opined the House should prove a sort of hornets' nest";
At least to turn it into one we've done our little best;
And though our pranks upon ourselves no credit seem to bring,
Still, when the Grand Old Man's our game—we're up to anything!
  We gibe at him like this, we snap at him like that;
    We yawn or laugh: sometimes we chaff, or contradict him flat;
      And, if he make a slip,
        We roar and yell and skip,

           And trust our brass may muster pass
              Somehow for Statesmanship!

If you should think our posturings our Party but degrade,
Reflect, "Our Party's" but ourselves, and we're all ready made:
Tact, reason, judgment to their work wise politicians bring,
But when the Grand Old Man's the butt—why, fools can have their
  fling.

Randolph Churchill and his 'Fourth Party' mocked Sir Stafford Northcote mercilessly in an attempt to sabotage his leadership of the party in the Commons. They thought his consensus politics too tepid – especially in opposition – and urged a sharper, more partisan approach.

HOW HAPPY WITH NEITHER!

THE LIBERAL NURSE: "I wish you had my brat." | THE CONSERVATIVE NURSE: "I wish you had mine."

Salisbury and Gladstone both had to contend with brilliant attackers within their own parties, and Randolph Churchill and Joe Chamberlain were often compared then and now. But Chamberlain's impact on the Liberals, the Conservatives and indeed the country was far more profound.

Joseph Chamberlain in Birmingham, 1903, persuasively arguing that his protectionist tariff would make no visible difference. Can you tell which loaf is bigger? he asked. But the difference in the Conservative party over free trade was visible enough, and all Balfour's manoeuvres could not paper over the divide.

Joseph Chamberlain always cared for principle more than party. Having left the Liberals over Irish Home Rule, he then contributed to the Conservative split over free trade.

FIDGETY JOE.

PAPA (D-KE OF D-V-NSH-RE).
    LET ME SEE IF JOSEPH CAN
    BE A LITTLE GENTLEMAN ;

MAMMA (ARTH-R B-LF-R).
    LET ME SEE IF HE IS ABLE
    TO SIT STILL FOR ONCE AT TABLE.
                Struwwelpeter adapted.

For such unprecedented transformations to take place without rebellion or revolution is remarkable; for them to take place without political controversy would have been impossible.

But beneath the changing issues that are the raw material of political debate, it is possible to identify three continuing sources of tension within the Conservative party. First, there is the inevitable strain, identified in Burke's famous phrase, between those who want to put the emphasis on conserving and those who want to put the emphasis on improving. Second, there is the continuing contrast in attitude between the paternalistic 'old' Tories and the 'liberal' strain. And third, there are the genuine disagreements over policies and personalities that appear in any demo cratic body representing a diversity of interests: the issue of free trade against tariff protection, for instance, that cracked the party in 1846, 1906 and 1912 and threatened it again in the 1920s; the quarrel over whether to end the Liberal–Conservative coalition in 1922; the bitter disagreement over appeasement in the 1930s, the serious division over Suez in 1956 and the rows over Rhodesia in the 1960s and 1970s.

The tension that has always existed between the 'conservers' and the 'improvers' serves a useful function as it forces the party to maintain a balance between conservation and change. From time to time one side or the other is ascendant, as were the conservers (they called them the 'diehards' and the 'ditchers') before the First World War, and the reformers in the years after the Second. The existence of the opposing wing has sooner or later always caused the balance to right itself.

The second contrast, between the 'old' Tories and the 'liberals' is in a way more interesting: the 'old' Tories see their roots stretching way back to a time of feudal community, when landlords and squires took responsibility for the poor, the homeless and the old of their district. Their historical vision may be more romantic than real, but the feeling it represents is genuine, and it underlay Disraeli's insistence on the

Violent scene in the House of Commons, 1911, when the Conservative 'die-hards' bellowed their opposition to Asquith's reforms. The party was deeply divided between 'die-hards' and moderates, a split not overcome until the war.

Bonar Law and J.C.C. Davidson
(party Chairman) leaving the Carlton
Club after the historic meeting of 19th
October 1922 when Austen
Chamberlain's leadership and the Lloyd
George coalition were toppled by a vote
of Conservative MPs.

obligations as well as the rights of ownership, and a century later Rab
Butler's insistence that it was part of the longest Conservative tradition
'that the majesty of the State might be used in the interests of the many'.

The 'liberal' strain is characterised by a passionate belief in individual
freedom, in equality of opportunity and by a profound distrust of over-
powerful, even if benign, government. The 'liberals' or 'radicals' in the
Tory party tend to believe with Burke, 'the greater the power the more
dangerous the abuse,' and also that 'government governs best which
governs least'.

In practice, of course, the 'old' Tory and 'liberal' strains have never
been sharply defined nor mutually exclusive. They commingle in the
party and often in individual MPs. They represent not a set of dogmas,
but rather attitudes of mind.

In addition to inevitable disagreements on philosophy and policies, the
party has had its share of leadership struggles, although considering the
number of ambitious and powerful personalities jostling for position,
coups and attempted coups have been extremely rare. Disraeli's attack on
Peel over the Corn Laws was a coup of sorts, and in the end Disraeli did
become Prime Minister, but Peel's downfall was compounded of far more
factors than Disraeli's assault. Randolph Churchill made a demogogic
attempt to take over the National Union in 1883 to use it as a platform to
take over the leadership, but he was outmanoeuvred by Lord Salisbury.

For the most part, however, competition for the Tory leadership has
been gentlemanly in the extreme. In 1911 Austen Chamberlain and Walter
Long, faced with the suggestion their rivalry might split the party, both
retired forthwith and let the unknown Bonar Law rise to the top. In 1922
Austen Chamberlain again, confronted with lack of support from the

backbenches, resigned immediately. His half-brother Neville, deposed as Prime Minister and succeeded by Churchill in 1940, was nonetheless allowed to continue as Conservative leader until his death several months later.

However, after the war, and after the gigantic figure of Churchill, leadership struggles became a bit sharper. The rival factions supporting Butler and Macmillan as successor to Eden made no secret of their advocacy, and many in the Butler camp were never reconciled. They lobbied for him with renewed vigour in 1963 when Macmillan's oddly timed resignation caused the party Conference, for the first and only time, to take on aspects of an American political convention. The gentlemanly tradition of graceful retirement resurfaced briefly when Alec Douglas-Home good humouredly stepped down following his defeat in 1964, but the next change in 1974–75 was fiercely fought.

This conflict, over Edward Heath's leadership, demonstrated the Tory dilemma when faced with a choice between loyalty to the leader (an enduring and powerful feature of Conservatism) and political pragmatism. Heath had led the party for a decade, fought four elections and lost three. To the unpopularity of electoral failure was added a growing, if ill-defined feeling that his brand of Conservatism was out of step with the mass of the party. Yet when the 1922 Committee extracted his promise to stand for re-selection as leader, it looked for a time as if none of his Parliamentary colleagues would challenge him. Margaret Thatcher was the first and, on the initial ballot, the only MP to announce as a candidate. It was an act of courage, according to the accounts of contemporary MPs, that decisively influenced the ultimate outcome. This leadership struggle, although short (November 1974 – February 1975) was very intense. It was about far more than the two personalities involved, and the final choice of Margaret Thatcher marked the fact the party wanted a sharp change of direction.

All these conflicts have taken place inside the party; in all its 150 years, there have been only two Conservative MPs who have stepped outside the party to become national figures on their own, and both did it over policy points, not as a ploy for personal power.

Winston Churchill took his lonely public stand against appeasement because he was totally convinced the party was set upon a course disastrous for the country.

Enoch Powell stepped outside the party in 1968 with his violent Birmingham speech against immigration. As a result of this speech Heath dismissed him from the Shadow Cabinet. *The Times* commented: 'the risk of having Mr Powell as an enemy . . . is less grave than having Mr Powell as a colleague.' Powell continued to make sensational and, to the Conservatives, damaging speeches which received extensive media coverage. In February 1974 he refused to stand for his Wolverhampton constituency as a Conservative and advised the nation to vote Labour. He was returned to Parliament in October 1974 as Ulster Unionist MP for Down South.

Although they became national figures, both Churchill and Powell were always each a single voice, never leaders of fully fledged factions. Churchill, of course, did not leave the party in the 1930s and returned from his self-imposed exile to become one of the greatest Conservative Prime Ministers.

The job of containing all the divergent strands of the Parliamentary party falls to the Whips. It is their task to create from the welter of passions and personalities a party capable of governing, or of providing effective opposition, and the growth in the importance of the Whips this

THE WOOLLY-MINDED TWINS: *'It's a positive outrage leaving the dear old homestead – AND FOR NO REASON WHATEVER!'*

Rearmament bitterly divided the party and the nation in the 1930s. Chamberlain and others with horrific memories of the 1914–18 conflict felt that a repeat of the terrible suffering must be avoided at all costs. Churchill and others believed the menace of Hitler had to be resisted. Poy cartoon from the Daily Mail, *1936.*

Changes in the leadership have always caused frictions in the party, but until 1963 the resolutions were always veiled from public view. Gabriel cartoon from the Daily Worker, *1953.*

century has paralleled the growth in governmental power. In the 19th century the role of government was very limited, and party discipline was very loose. With the extension of the franchise, governments had election promises to keep and legislative programmes to enact. To do it they needed consistent backbench support, and the 1880s, 1890s and early 1900s were a time of struggle for control of the Parliamentary party. The Whips were the instrument appointed by the leadership to exercise this control, and they used, according to Robert Wallace, MP in 1895, 'a dexterous blending of menace, cajolery and reward'. 'On any signs of individual action in their party,' said Wallace, 'they can put the pistol of Dissolution to their heads and say, "Your vote or your life; if you do not come to heel, we will blow your Parliamentary brains out."'

Not that it always worked: a contemporary observer described the scene in 1905 when the backbenchers refused to support the Balfour administration: 'Old fashioned Tories . . . now left the House swearing that nothing would induce them to stay and vote. They swept past the Whips at the doors, ignoring their presence or rudely repelling their efforts to detain them, till the Whips themselves deserted their posts in despair . . .'

The party leadership, through the Whips, did in the end gain control, and party discipline in the 20th century has been much tighter. It has to be: 20th-century governments could not get through the workload expected of them without a united party. It is now relatively rare for a Conservative MP to defy the Whip on a crucial matter of party policy. The unanimity is accomplished not so much by pressure from the Whips' office as by a

Sir Anthony Eden addresses the 22 nation Suez Conference, 16th August 1956. The Anglo-French action in Egypt provoked a furious intra- as well as inter-party clash. For the first time since 1924 a sitting in the House had to be suspended, several members of the government resigned, and MPs were attacked for their stand by their constituency associations.

sense that non-support would be 'letting the side down'. The gulf that separates the two main parties in the last part of the 20th century is much wider than the one that separated 19th-century parties, and MPs take themselves and their job altogether more seriously.

Disunity, of course, besides being a hindrance to effective government and opposition, is a serious electoral handicap, as the Conservatives have discovered both to their cost and to their benefit. Disunity and internal divisions were important factors in keeping them out of power from 1846 to 1866, and in their catastrophic defeat in 1906. Disunity in the Liberal party, however, was a major factor in Conservative victories between 1886 and 1902, and dissension in the Labour party had some part to play in Tory electoral success in the 1950s. These memories, particularly when recalled by the Whips, have a calming effect on dissenting MPs.

It is also true that discord makes better headlines than harmony, and newspapers are guilty of exaggerating the natural diversity of all parties, and spotlighting as 'splits' what are only common or garden differences of opinion.

Outside Parliament, in the national party, disagreements have also always existed, more usually over policy than over philosophy. Baldwin complained that 'Leading the party is like driving pigs to market,' but the disagreements have in fact been generally muted and veiled from the public eye. It is partly a matter of style: Conservatives tend to be people who were taught that open dispute is bad manners. It has already been

Lord Hailsham (Quintin Hogg) and R.A. Butler on the Conference platform in Blackpool, 1963. They were the front-runners with Reginald Maudling for the leadership when Macmillan resigned, but Sir Alec Douglas-Home turned out to be the party's choice. The struggle, conducted publicly at the Conference, was unprecedented and led to the introduction of a ballot procedure.

Edward Heath and Margaret Thatcher shake hands at the Conservative Conference in Brighton, 1978. Among Conservatives allegiance to the party in the long run transcends personality clashes.

noted that Conservative conferences are more convivial than controversial, a fact that causes grumbling among news reporters. In his closing speech to the 1948 Conference Lord Woolton said, with a hint of satisfaction, 'There has been no clash of opinion here . . . The Press must have found us perhaps a little dull . . .' Thirty years later reporters were still saying the unity of Conservative conferences made boring copy.

There is, in fact, a multitude of different groups within the national party, but it would be a mistake to see them as factions – indeed, many of them were initiated and are supported by Central Office: Young Conservatives, Federation of Conservative Students, Conservative Trade Unionists, Women's Advisory Committee, Conservative Political Centre. There are also other special interest 'pressure' groups which rise and fall with the temper of the times: the Bow Group, PEST (Pressure for Economic and Social Toryism), the Monday Club, the Tory Reform Group. These offer a platform to the different strands within the party and are important forums for the airing of competing views, but none sees itself as a challenge to the leadership.

If there were not a variety of views within the Conservative party it would contrast oddly with their oft-stated belief in pluralism, diversity and the 'free marketplace of ideas'. 'Conservatives have never believed they have a monopoly of truth,' said Lord Hailsham, an important shaper of contemporary Conservative thought, and went on to counsel: 'When, therefore, they are asked what their party stands for, Conservatives would do well to begin their answer by saying "variety" . . .'

CHAPTER 8
Social Reform

In 1947, during the period of the first full-term Labour government, one of their spokesmen accused the Conservatives of supporting the contemporary welfare legislation only out of 'me-tooism' and claimed they were secretly planning to dismantle it later.

Whereupon Lord Hailsham (then Quintin Hogg) lost his temper: 'A party,' he snapped back, 'which pioneered factory reform, completed the legalising of trade unions, founded public health administration and workmen's compensation, introduced the contributory pensions scheme, launched the slum clearance campaigns, started the milk-in-schools scheme and used its majority to pass all the great operative Education Acts of this century, may be forgiven if it brands both kinds of criticism as impudent, ignorant and shallow.'

This exchange reveals an interesting modern paradox: the Conservative party has, in fact, initiated and passed more social reform legislation than any other party, yet today they are believed by many people to be opposed to the welfare state and antagonistic to reform. Why?

It is probably because, having waged and won the titanic 19th-century battle to establish the principle of government action to improve social conditions, the Conservatives let their reforming zeal flag in the 1890s, and allowed their 'Die-Hard' wing to dominate in the early 1900s. Therefore in these crucial years they lost the propaganda initiative; the image (so central to 20th-century politics) of the 'progressive' party passed first to the Liberals and then to the Labour party, and the Tories, despite three strikingly reformist administrations, have not yet gained it back.

The roots of the situation are these. The 18th-century industrial revolution affected Britain like an earthquake, shattering completely the old world and leaving the landscape wholly changed. The 19th century was heir to its evils and its benefits, both scattered indiscriminately, and thought by many to be inextricably intermixed. It was believed that the benefits would not exist without the evils – that factories, railroads, expanding empire and increasing national wealth could not exist without brutal exploitation in the mines and savagely long hours in the mills. Any restriction on the untrammelled exercise of enterprise would damage, so it was thought, the dynamic that had created the explosion of progress and prosperity that was the most visible feature of Victorian England.

This was the doctrine called 'laissez-faire', endorsed by the 'classical' economists such as Adam Smith and given credence by the personal experiences of entrepreneurs whose rags to riches stories were a staple of Victorian folklore. Throughout the 19th century the battle raged to humanise this doctrine. Sir Robert Peel, ceaselessly harried by the Tory reformer Lord Ashley, enacted in 1842 the first major legislation dealing with exploitation in the mining industry and, in 1844, an act limiting the working hours of women and children. In 1845 Peel created the Board of Supervision, the forerunner of the Ministry of Health.

In doing this Peel established the precedent that the state could take

The Derby–Disraeli Reform Act of 1867 doubled the electorate and gave votes to the working class for the first time. Many Tories were extremely dubious, and Lord Derby himself described it as a 'leap in the dark'.

Early 'Peeler' or 'Bobbie': law and order is a consistent Conservative theme. Sir Robert Peel founded the metropolitan police (hence the nicknames) in 1829, and as Home Secretary in the 1820s fundamentally revised and simplified the criminal code.

The cartoonist George Cruikshank drew this as a powerful protest against the number of people being hanged for passing forged Bank of England notes. Indeed, before 1830, people were executed for lesser offences than that. Peel drastically reduced the number of crimes that carried the death penalty.

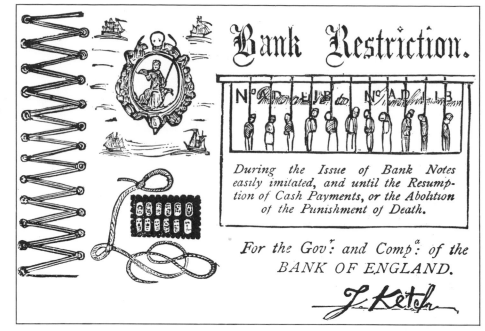

'Capital & Labour', a Punch cartoon of 1843. Disraeli in his novels and through the group 'Young England' attacked this disparity between Victorian rich and poor, and in particular the exploitative conditions in factories and mines. He also attacked Peel's government for insufficient social action.

Sweated labour in the 1840s. Conditions in Victorian factories were rotten, and throughout the century Parliament struggled to improve them. Peel's 1844 Factory Bill limited working hours (not enough, said Disraeli and Lord Shaftesbury; too much, said the Liberal John Bright). Subsequently Disraeli passed more legislation on factory conditions and hours of work in 1866, 1867 and 1874.

The main staircase in the Carlton Club.

1909

1909

190

Fifty years of posters from the Conservative archives.

1931

1935

1935

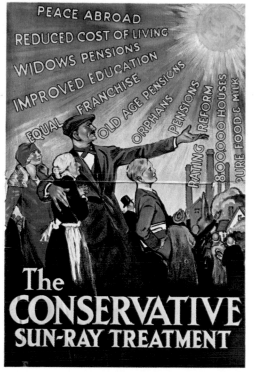

1929

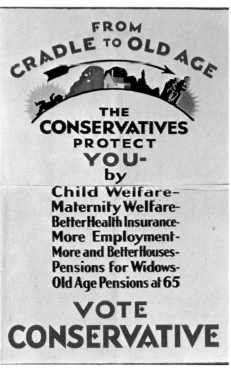

1929

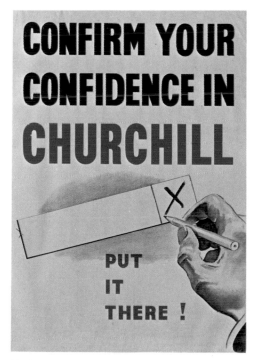

1945

1959

The House of Lords.

action to better the conditions of the people: intervene in industry to the extent of setting regulations and take positive action in the field of public health. It was established in the face of fierce and bitter resistance from people – represented in Parliament mainly by the Liberal party – who sincerely believed economic ruin and moral decline would be the result of government interference in industry and in the conditions of private life.

Disraeli reinforced the precedent and moved forward the idea of state action for social welfare. Having stated unequivocally that one of the three objects of the Tory party was the 'elevation of the condition of the people', he proceeded during his 1874–80 administration to pass legislation for the improvement of public health, the purity of food and drugs, the protection of merchant seamen and the right of trade unions to peacefully strike. His administration put through an act giving power to local authorities to clear slums and build new dwellings, and another act making elementary education compulsory throughout the country.

Almost equally important for the shape of 20th-century Britain was Peel's peacetime income tax, which established the precedent of progressive taxation – taxing according to means – in order to pay for the needs of society as a whole.

The springs of these 19th-century Conservative reforms were three. First, the old paternalistic Tory tradition, people whose deepest feelings were outraged by the squalor, inhumanity and degradation produced by the industrial revolution. Their personal family traditions of responsibility, stemming from 'feudal paternalism' and 'noblesse oblige', convinced them it was the duty of the state to remedy these conditions. Delegations of these Tories came to lobby Peel on the necessity of factory legislation. Disraeli, in his novel *Sybil*, published in 1845, wrote with passion about the unbearable conditions in mines and mills, and put his famous 'two nation' passage into the mouth of Sybil's lover: 'Yes . . . [the Queen reigns over] two nations between whom there is no intercourse and no sympathy – who are as ignorant of each other's habits, thoughts and feelings as if they were dwellers in different zones or inhabitants of different planets – who are formed by a different breeding, are fed by a different food, and are ordered by different manners, and are not governed by the same laws . . . THE RICH AND THE POOR.'

The second spring of 19th-century Conservative social reform was Christian evangelism, whose chief exponent was the Tory peer Lord Ashley, later Earl of Shaftesbury. Impatient, determined, single-minded, utterly dedicated to social improvement, Ashley was the moving spirit behind the mining legislation, the shorter working hours acts, the regulation of common lodging houses (described by Charles Dickens as 'the best measure ever passed in Parliament'). It was Ashley who founded the Ragged School Movement for the wild orphans of the London streets, and it was his personal campaign to save the 'climbing boys' that finally ended this sad business of sending small children to sweep the towering Victorian flues. The secular 20th century finds it hard to believe in the intensity of the Victorian religious sense, but as an influence for social reform it cannot be underestimated.

The third spring of 19th-century Conservative social reform was the pressure of the enlarged electorate. Disraeli enfranchised a sizeable new group with the 1867 act, and the party began immediately to campaign for their support. The material produced by Central Office throughout the last part of the century prominently features appeals and commitments to 'the working man'.

But under Lord Salisbury and subsequently his nephew Arthur Balfour the pace of Conservative reform slackened. Salisbury was not an

Ashley Cooper, Lord Shaftesbury, key figure in 19th-century social reform. His politics were Conservative, but the mainspring of his actions was Christian evangelism. His personal pressure was instrumental in legislation on factories, mines, child labour, working hours, supervision of common lodging houses and reform of the lunacy laws. He also founded the Ragged Schools.

Life in Golden Lane, 1872. In 1868 Disraeli had appointed a Royal Commission on the sanitary laws; in the famous 1872 Manchester Speech he pointed to the need for health and sanitary legislation ('Sanitas sanitatum, omnia sanitas'), and in 1875 he passed the Public Health Act.

Cheapside in the 1890s. 19th-century England's population was transformed from primarily rural to overwhelmingly urban. Lord Salisbury's local government legislation underpinned the development of 20th-century towns and cities. 'The object of local government,' he told the National Union in 1887, 'is to diminish central government. The object of local government is to place in the hands of the people of the locality the power hitherto exercised by departments in London.'

Slums in 19th-century Westminster. Slums proliferated as cities swelled. Richard Cross, Home Secretary under Disraeli, put through Housing Acts that were the first to authorise slum clearance, empowering local authorities to condemn, demolish and reconstruct whole areas.

enthusiast for excessive state action. He said once (apropos of Ireland, but revealing of his outlook): 'The optimist view of politics assumes that there must be some remedy for every political ill, and rather than not find it, will make two hardships to cure one . . . But is not the other view barely possible? Is it not just conceivable that there is no remedy that we can apply . . .?'

Despite this pessimism about political panaceas, Salisbury did believe in the beneficial effects of good administration and the wisdom of decentralised power. It was during his administration that the local government structure was created which has had such an impact, though often unnoticed, on the shape of 20th-century Britain.

It was also during Salisbury's time as leader of the party that Joseph Chamberlain, the famous Birmingham radical Liberal, joined the Tories in protest over Gladstone's proposed Irish Home Rule. With him came a large group of Liberal Unionists, whose energetic ideas of how society might be improved were an important long-term gain for the Conservative party. Harold Macmillan's political ancestry, for example, was Liberal Unionist. Although popular to the point of demagoguery in his own time, Joe Chamberlain's actual legacy is slight compared to that of his son Neville, who became one of the next century's most imaginative and progressive politicians.

Arthur Balfour followed Salisbury as Prime Minister, and the pace of social reform slowed further, with disastrous results for the party. Although the seminal Education Act of 1902 was passed, as was the Unemployed Workmen Act (which set up local distress committees to help find jobs for the out of work), Balfour's administration was basically unresponsive to the demands of his time. This was dramatically illustrated by the rapid growth of the newly born Labour party and was a major cause of the electoral disaster of 1906, when the Conservatives were reduced to 157, and Balfour himself lost his seat. He returned to Parliament shortly after in a by-election, but during the next years he

St George British School, Bristol, 1895. By the end of the 19th century elementary education was universal, but with patchy standards and confused organisation. The 1902 Education Act reorganised the entire system, putting all elementary schools on the rates and under the control of a local authority education committee. It was one of Balfour's few genuine achievements and ironically cost him innumerable votes.

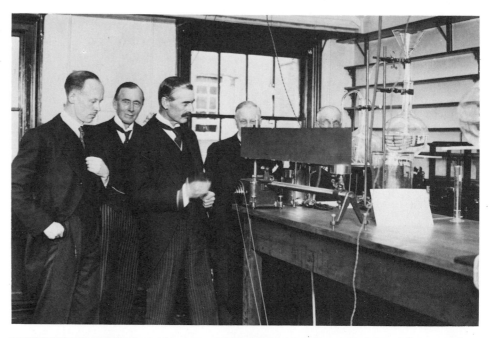

Neville Chamberlain opens a new laboratory at the Pharmaceutical Society, June 1926. As Minister of Health, 1924–29, Chamberlain was an important shaper of the Welfare State, putting through legislation on pensions, housing, health and unemployment.

Captain Ian Fraser, the blind Conservative MP, with 'new' voters on polling day, 1929. The 1928 Act passed by Baldwin's government gave even 'flappers' (ie women under 30) the vote.

participated in a policy of obstruction of Liberal reform legislation that culminated in the battle of the 1909 budget: the House of Lords, in the face of 250 years of Parliamentary precedent, refused to pass the budget, with the ultimate result that their House was castrated by the Parliament Act of 1911.

It was 1924 before the Conservatives took power again for a full term. During this administration Neville Chamberlain, as Minister of Health, put through a series of interconnected reforms designed to create a 'circle of security', including subsidised house building, pensions for widows and orphans, public health measures, unemployment insurance, national health insurance and a reform of the out-dated Poor Laws. Baldwin, Prime Minister during those years, encouraged these measures. 'I have always,' he said once, 'endeavoured to make the Conservative party face left in its anti-socialism.'

The Conservative-dominated National government wrestled with the intractable problem of unemployment throughout the 1930s, but with very limited success. Their failure to solve it was an important element in the massive defeat of 1945.

In 1940 Winston Churchill became Prime Minister, following Neville

Chamberlain. The 1935 election had returned 432 Conservatives, 154 Labour and 30 'other' MPs, and as elections were suspended during the war, this was the basic shape of the parliament until 1945. Churchill invited several Labour leaders to join the War Cabinet so as to present a united national image during the years of crisis. It was, however, essentially a Conservative government, greatly influenced by Rab Butler, which laid the outlines of post-war social legislation: the White Paper on the National Health Service was published in March 1944; the plan for implementing the main recommendations of the Beveridge Report on social security (including family allowances) was published in 1944; the Education Act reforming the structure of state education was passed in 1944. Most of the legislation outlined in the White Papers was subsequently enacted by the Labour government (1945–51), with the support of the Conservative party.

All this was very much in the tradition of the Tory reformers of the 19th century. The dominant element had always been a desire to work towards 'the correction of proved abuses and the redress of real grievances' (as Peel said in the Tamworth Manifesto) and towards healing the divide between Disraeli's 'two nations'. But there had always been another strand in the Conservative attitude towards social reform, one which was voiced by Edmund Burke in 1791, when contemplating the reforming programme of the French revolutionists: 'Individuality is left out of their scheme of government. The state is all in all . . . The state has dominion and conquest for its sole objects – dominion over minds by proselytism, over bodies by arms.'

This strand – an understanding that there were dangers to individual freedom inherent in the expansion of government power – has always existed in Conservative thought. It held a kind of 'watching brief' throughout the time when a civilised conscience demanded state action to remedy unbearable social evils. It surfaced from time to time – for instance in the smart dismissal of the idea (during the enthusiasm for public hygiene that came with the discovery of germs) that state inspectors be allowed to enter private homes and inspect the sanitary arrangements. John Stuart Mill spoke to this strand of Conservative thought when he said, 'The sole end for which mankind are warranted, individually or collectively, in interfering with the liberty of action of any of their number is self-protection.'

Squatters demonstrate in Regents Park, 1946. The post-war housing crisis was acute and led to the 1950 Conservative Conference (most unusually) demanding a pledge from Ministers to build 300,000 houses. Later Macmillan as Minister of Housing exceeded the target.

Edward Heath as Minister of Labour in 1960 with Lord Beveridge to mark the 50th anniversary of Employment Exchanges. William Beveridge's seminal report on Social Insurance and Allied Services published in 1942 was received in Parliament without a single Conservative dissenting.

As the 20th century opened and proceeded, George Orwell touched the same chord with his terrifying vision of bureaucratic tyranny in *1984*. But it was Winston Churchill who was the first modern Tory leader to give voice, with characteristic pungency, to this strand in Conservative thought: 'We do not wish the people of this ancient island reduced to a mass of State-directed proletariats, thrown hither and thither, housed here and there, by an aristocracy of privileged officials or privileged party, sectarian or trade union bosses.'

The re-emergence of this fundamental belief – that individual freedom must be protected against any concentration of power, including the monopoly power of the state – has had great influence on Conservative thought since the war. If the foundation of the Conservative attitude toward social reform is, as Disraeli stated it, 'the elevation of the condition of the people', Tories believed this could be best effected by state action in the years 1830–1945. Since 1945, however, the Conservative attitude has shifted to a conviction that the 'condition of the people' would be best elevated by halting the extension of state action and reinvigorating the idea of individual action.

This, according to Lord Hailsham, reflects the most enduring of Conservative traits – to redress the balance in society by leaning against the current orthodoxy, whether it be 19th-century laissez-faire or 20th-century state control.

'Set the People Free' was the slogan of the successful Conservative campaign in 1951, and in the following thirteen years of Conservative administrations steps were taken to redress the balance of power in favour

Old age pensioners march to Buckingham Palace, 1973, after spending the night camped outside the home of the Minister for Social Services, in a 'national demonstration of concern'. Social reform in the 19th century owed much to impassioned individuals like Shaftesbury. In the 20th it owes more to an enlarged and increasingly articulate electorate.

Margaret Thatcher during a visit to a Blackpool school, 1975. During the same year she stated her own Conservative approach to social reform: 'Let our children grow tall – and some grow taller than others, if they have it in them to do so. We must build a society in which each citizen can develop his full potential, both for his own benefit and for the community as a whole . . . in which we encourage, rather than restrict the variety and richness of human nature.'

of the individual, with, for example, cuts in personal taxation, the removal of wartime controls, a programme to extend home ownership, the expansion of private funded pension schemes and anti-monopoly legislation.

However, the idea that 'social reform' should now mean an increase in personal freedom rather than an increase in state action has had a mixed reception. 'Set the people free' was very popular in 1951, and the steadily increasing affluence of the decade (which Tories with some justification claim was a result of their policies) made it more popular still. Then the economic troubles of the 1960s and 1970s revived demands for state action. ('In a contest between ease and liberty,' gloomily observed Lord Halifax long ago, 'the first hath generally prevailed.')

But the Conservatives fought and won the 1979 election on a clearly stated platform of less goverment action and more individual freedom. 'In our philosophy,' explained Margaret Thatcher in Zürich in 1977, 'the purpose of the life of the individual is not to be the servant of the state and its objectives, but to make the best of his talents and qualities. The sense of being self-reliant, of playing a role within the family, of owning one's own property, of paying one's way, are all part of the spiritual ballast which maintains responsible citizenship and provides the solid foundation from which people look around to see what more they might do, for others and for themselves.'

CHAPTER 9
Foreign Affairs

FOR MOST of the 19th century the sun shone on Britain's relations with the outside world. True, the century started with the Napoleonic wars and was immediately preceded by the shock of the French revolution; but Wellington did triumph over Napoleon, and the French revolution had the salutary effect – for the Conservatives – of solidifying support behind their embryo party.

After Waterloo, however, most Britons turned their attention to their own absorbing political and economic events. The foreign relations that were conducted had the feel of a family affair: Queen Victoria was related to virtually all the crowned heads of Europe; British politicians of every party were drawn from the privileged classes, who as a matter of course toured the capitals of Europe when young and holidayed in European resorts throughout their lives. Peel was actually in Italy when the summons came to head the government in 1834. It took well over a week just to locate him, and another fortnight for him to get back to London, which gives an insight into the different pace of 19th-century affairs.

Foreign ministers of all political flavours saw their job as primarily to keep the peace, to preserve the balance of power in Europe and to maintain Britain's satisfyingly dominant position in the world. Then in the 1870s this relatively limited view began to change. Three irresistible forces were at work, and it is a measure of Disraeli's political genius that he floated the idea of Empire (in his famous Crystal Palace speech in June 1872) at precisely the moment when these forces began to be felt.

First, it was just then that the balance of power in Europe suddenly shifted. Germany and Italy had been off the world stage, engrossed in their struggles for national unity, for years. In 1871 both finally became unified and were immediately a potential threat to the dominance Britain had enjoyed since Waterloo.

Second, Victorian industry – grown from its raw beginnings in the 18th century to a colossus representing huge investments in plant, machinery and labour – badly needed new markets and guaranteed supplies of raw materials, especially now that it was faced for the first time with serious competition from Germany and America.

Third, mass education and wholesale urbanisation, both just beginning in the 1870s, were about to create a huge army of people who had been freed from the drudgery of labour on the land only to be incarcerated in dingy offices as typists, bank clerks, shop assistants and minor civil servants. People who spent six days a week in cramped Dickensian offices, who went home at night to pinched terrace houses in mean suburban streets, who still spent most of Sunday on the hard pews of Victorian churches – these were the people who hungered for the romance of Empire, who bought Rudyard Kipling's poems by the hundred thousand, and read with longing about 'the road to Mandalay, where the flyin'-fishes play, An' the dawn comes up like thunder outer China 'crost the bay!'

Whether Disraeli had identified these three forces is not known, but

Cartoon shows Edmund Burke loosing his wrath on the vicar who dared endorse the French Revolution. Burke's reactions to this foreign event, published in Reflections on the Revolution in France, *had a profound effect on the embryo Conservative party.*

John Bull's attitude here to the combatants in the American Civil War summed up the 19th-century British attitude to foreign affairs: "We don't care what you do as long as it doesn't interfere with us.'

JOHN BULL'S NEUTRALITY.
"LOOK HERE, BOYS, I DON'T CARE TWOPENCE FOR YOUR NOISE; BUT IF YOU THROW STONES AT MY WINDOWS, I MUST THRASH YOU BOYS"

given their existence the idea of Empire was a political winner. And for a long time it worked. Britain stayed among the richest and most powerful nations in the world despite heavyweight competition from Germany and the US; and the images of Empire brought vivid colour to the closing years of the century. There is a school of thought that claims the mass of people never cared for the Empire, but the gigantic sales of writers like Rider Haggard as well as Kipling, the tremendous enthusiasm for the 'Colonials' at Victoria's jubilees, and the wild scenes of jubilation on Mafeking night indicate otherwise.

Disraeli gave the idea of Empire an important fillip when he had Queen Victoria crowned Empress of India in 1876, and thus invested the monarchy (and by implication the nation) with the glamour of a world-wide empire.

Disraeli had two other notable successes in the field of foreign affairs: in 1875 he pipped the French by purchasing the Khedive of Egypt's shares in the Suez canal; and in 1878 he staged a successful sabre-rattling exercise that halted Russia's threatened war with Turkey. At the subsequent Congress of Berlin he acquired Cyprus for the Empire and arrived home

to find he was the toast of all England, credited with preserving the peace
of Europe.

It was after Disraeli's death, in the 1890s, that the idea of Empire
reached its spectacularly raucous peak, urged on by the impassioned
brilliance of Joe Chamberlain as Colonial Secretary under Lord Salisbury.
Chamberlain, according to Winston Churchill, 'was incomparably the
most live, sparkling, insurgent, compulsive figure in British affairs . . .'
His vision of Imperial Britain gripped the imagination of the party and the
country, the red marks of British dominance spread across the maps in
every schoolroom and the new half-penny press chronicled the saga of
exploration and exploitation in Africa, China and the Middle East with
feverish enthusiasm.

But the 'Imperial Vision' was flawed; not all the party – certainly not
Lord Salisbury – shared Chamberlain's grandiose ambitions, and even
then the 'winds of change' – described by Harold Macmillan 60 years later
– were beginning to blow. Macmillan was the Conservative leader
destined to complete the transformation of Empire into Commonwealth
and of colonies into self-governing nations, a process that was foreshadowed, even while the Empire was at its height, by the Colonial
Conferences of the 1890s. It was a process that particularly engaged the
Conservative party, just as the original creation of Empire had done. It
was not accomplished without trauma.

There were always those in the party who saw in the Empire more than
a factor in the European power balance, a collection of guaranteed
markets or a source of escapist literature. There were many who believed
that the peace and affluence of Victorian Britain laid upon them an
obligation to help others reach an equally favoured state, and that the
Empire was more a responsibility than a resource, to which they owed at
the least education, health care and efficient administration.

This sense of responsibility – the 'white man's burden' – is out of
fashion now, but it unquestionably spurred thousands of people to spend
large parts of their lives in jungles, deserts, primitive hospitals and
missionary schoolrooms trying to bring the 'benefits of civilisation' to the
outposts of Empire.

It was this sense of responsibility, as well as a reluctance to relinquish
Britain's world role, that fuelled the 20th-century conflict in the party
over granting self-government to the former colonies. The conflict was

Advertisement, June 1893: besides glamour and romance, imperialism had a solid commercial base. British business needed markets far from European and US tariffs; British manufacturers needed raw materials. To the Empire builders it appeared merely common sense to secure both under the British flag.

Colonial troops in England for Queen Victoria's Diamond Jubilee celebrations. It was Joseph Chamberlain's idea that this Jubilee should celebrate the 'Imperial Family Under the British Crown', and some 3 million people poured into London to do so.

The fourth Colonial Conference, 1902, with Joseph Chamberlain in the centre. It was a disappointment to those pursuing the Imperial Dream – the colonies·were not enthusiastic about subordinating their interests for the 'mother country'.

The original caption which appeared with this magazine illustration ('Administrators of Empire at their work of spreading peace, law and order in remotest Africa') reflects the sincere view held by many who supported the Empire that they had a duty to share the benefits of British law, justice and administration, and that it was wicked to renege on this responsibility. Churchill was such a one and was outraged at the prospect of Britain relinquishing the Empire.

Low's comment on the Locarno Pact, 1925. Between the wars politicians made real attempts to cement a lasting peace. Austen Chamberlain (as Foreign Secretary) was the moving force behind the Treaty of Locarno – a non-aggression pact between France, Germany and Belgium – and it was regarded as his greatest achievement. He himself called it 'the real dividing line between the years of war and the years of peace.'

Imperial Conference, October 1923, at 10 Downing St. Baldwin (legs crossed) in the centre, Lord Curzon fourth from left, General Smuts fourth from the right. It was Baldwin by his policy towards India who set in train the actual end of Empire and the beginning of Commonwealth.

particularly bitter over India; Churchill actually resigned from the Shadow Cabinet in 1931 over what he called 'this frightful prospect'. There were many Conservatives who agreed with him, who saw the retreat from Empire as an abdication of responsibility.

There was also for many years a nagging sense that 'something more' might be made of the Empire. Joe Chamberlain had had a vision of Imperial economic union, with Britain and her colonies linked and safe behind towering tariff walls. The press lords Beaverbrook and Rothermere resurrected this idea in the aftermath of the 1929 Conservative election defeat and in the face of approaching world depression. In these conditions their 'United Empire Party' attracted considerable support, but it fizzled when Baldwin pointed out that the great Dominions had no intention of participating.

That was the last important appearance of the 'Imperial Dream'. In 1931 the Statute of Westminster gave legal backing to the 'Dominion' status for former colonies that had been agreed at the 1926 Imperial Conference, and the scene was set for the final act. When Alec Douglas-Home took over as Secretary of State for Commonwealth Relations in 1955, he said: 'I was able to read the signs of evolutionary change. Empire was finished; the

Churchill meets Truman at Potsdam, 17th July 1945. The British General Election had been held, 5th July, but the results were not announced until 26th July. At Potsdam, therefore, Churchill was in reality no longer Prime Minister.

Like the French Revolution more than a century before, the Russian Revolution had an important effect on both the Conservative party and British domestic affairs. Again, there was widespread fear of a foreign-inspired revolution. The 'Zinoviev letter', published fortuitously on the eve of the 1924 election, played upon it.

1955: the Indian Premier Jawaharlal Nehru arrives in London. Anthony Eden, who had become PM barely two months before, talks to Nehru's daughter, Indira Gandhi. The transition of India from colony to self-governing nation caused immense traumas in the Conservative party.

Some said the 'great expedition' to Suez was a last imperial fling; others that it was a 'collective aberration'. It caused bitter divisions in the Conservative party and in the country and was a vivid object lesson on the changed position of Britain in the world.

IT'S ON—AND EDEN STICKS TO HIS GUNS!

THE invasion is on—in a blackout. Sir Anthony Eden confirmed it in the Commons yesterday, but refused to give one detail of British or French military movements.

"We stand by our decision," he told the angry Opposition.

As the world waited for news, only rumours from foreign radio stations broke the silence.

One concrete fact was a Ministry of Defence statement that: "All available means, including broadcasting, are being used to inform the Egyptian people as follows:

"'All civilians in Egypt are warned for their safety to keep away from all Egyptian airfields from now onwards until the Egyptian Government accepts the request of the United Kingdom and French Governments delivered on October 30.'"

Asked to elaborate the statement, a Ministry spokesman said it was "an operational announcement."

About the reference to "airfields," the spokesman said: "We are warning civilians. Any military force would be foolish to give its plans away."

Mr. Hugh Gaitskell, the Socialist Leader, announced in the Commons a censure motion on the Government and all constitutional opposition to its policy in the Middle East.

Sir Anthony called the U.S. resolution in the Security Council "in effect, a condemnation of Israel as the aggressor."

"We felt that we could not associate ourselves with this and we said so through diplomatic channels both in London and New York," he said.

● 'Prisoners captured'

"Is there any member of this House who can consider Egypt as an innocent country who can be exonerated at the Security Council by condemning Israel as an aggressor?" Sir Anthony asked.

Israeli troops were continuing to advance towards the Canal, and the latest report was that they were approaching the Canal.

"There have been a number of prisoners captured, I understand," said Sir Anthony.

"In the light of these facts can anybody say that we or the French Government should have waited?"

"We have no desire whatever, nor have the French Government, that the military action we shall have to take should be more than temporary in its duration.

"But it is our intention that our action to protect the Canal and separate the combatants should result in a settlement which will prevent such a situation arising periodically in the future.

"In the actions we have taken, we are not concerned to stop Egypt, but to stop war."

→ *Back Page*

modern Commonwealth could not be a military alliance nor an economic
bloc; if it was to remain a recognisable entity it would have to be a
political association, the members of which had decided that on balance it
was better to face the problems of the complex modern world together
rather than separately.'

In the years that followed some 30 remaining colonies were granted
independence and became self-governing members of the Commonwealth, which in 1978 comprised 36 member countries with a combined
population of more than 900 million. The terms on which this was
accomplished were hammered out by the Macmillan administration; and
the achievement of so much independence with so little conflict stands as
one of the wonders of contemporary diplomacy.

In areas of foreign affairs other than the Empire and Commonwealth,
Britain's position in this century is in stark contrast to her position in the
last. In the 19th century Britain dominated the world, secure behind an
undefeated navy, rich in possessions overseas and full of confidence and
productivity at home. Perhaps because the Conservative party was so
intimately involved in the expansion and success of the 19th century, it
has found it particularly difficult to reconcile itself to the diminished
circumstances of the 20th. Churchill, certainly, was unreconciled: 'I have
not become the King's First Minister,' he said in 1942, 'in order to preside
over the liquidation of the British Empire.'

However, even as the old century ended and the new began, it was
apparent realities had changed. The Boer War revealed British military
and naval capability was seriously outdated and her position in the world
dangerously isolated and exposed. It is to the credit of Arthur Balfour,
Prime Minister at the time, that he immediately entered into a series of

international alliances aimed at safeguarding British interests, set up the Committee of Imperial Defence and initiated a complete overhaul of the army and navy.

It is, in fact, these two themes – as typified by Balfour's quest for national security and Churchill's refusal to accept a reduced role despite reduced means – that have marked the Conservative attitude to foreign affairs throughout the 20th century. They underlie the continuing Conservative desire to strengthen NATO and to secure the American relationship; they were behind Macmillan's determined attempts to realise an East–West detente, and they are important factors in the Conservative commitment to the EEC.

It was Edward Heath who took the country into the EEC, but it was Harold Macmillan who first persuaded the Conservative party that Britain should apply. It was not easy: the Conservative attachment to national sovereignty is one of the party's most enduring features. But another, even stronger, is a devotion to British interests, and from their earliest beginnings the Tories have always pragmatically believed that the national interest is the prime determinate of foreign policy. Peel pointed out in 1844: 'The great art of government is to work by such instruments as the world supplies.' And Macmillan, urging the application to the EEC, pointed out with equal candour: 'Supposing we stand outside . . . of course we shall go on, but we shall be relatively weak, and we shan't find the true strength that we have and ought to have. We shan't be able to exercise it in a world of giants.'

But there was more to it than that; many Conservatives have a larger vision of the European community. The journalist Anthony Sampson described it when he said Macmillan 'was keenly aware of the need to provide both for the Government and for the nation a focus of policy and aspiration that was different from the Empire of the past but greater than Britain and her domestic problems. Europe therefore became for Macmillan the hope that would inspire future generations as the Empire had inspired the past . . .'

The Conservative policy document *The Right Approach*, published in 1977, endorsed this view, and said that in foreign affairs the party's strategy was 'to maintain Britain's security and interests, and to increase her influence abroad, not least through a whole-hearted contribution to the development of the European Community'.

Sir Alec Douglas-Home in the White House with President Kennedy, 4th October 1963. Home was Foreign Secretary then; a fortnight later he was to be Prime Minister.

RESPONSIBILITY - PROGRESS

The 1962 Conservative party
Conference at Llandudno voting for their
government's Common Market
proposals. To persuade the party, the
proposals were presented as supplements
to continued commitment to the
Commonwealth and the special
relationship with the US; de Gaulle saw
this as half-hearted commitment to
Europe and vetoed Britain's application
to join.

23rd January 1972: Prime Minister
Edward Heath signs the official
document making Britain a member of
the EEC. Sir Alec Douglas-Home is on
his right, Geoffrey Rippon on his left.

CHAPTER 10
At War

IN 1878, while Disraeli was ostentatiously readying the British troops for possible action against Russia, a certain bellicose jingle was being sung in all the music halls:

We don't want to fight, but, by jingo if we do,
We've got the ships, we've got the men, we've got the money too.

There is no one now in Britain who would sing such a ditty, not just because it is no longer true, but because the intervening years – the 'century of total war' – have caused a total revulsion, in the Conservative party as everywhere else, against the holocaust of modern war.

From the serene complacency created by decades of peace (broken only by faraway conflicts at the fringes of the Empire), the 19th century could – and did – contemplate war as a glorious adventure. Winston Churchill, as a little boy in the 1880s, lined up his ranks of gorgeously uniformed toy soldiers and thought 'it would be splendid to command an Army.'

He, along with nearly half a million others, sailed off to fight the Boers in South Africa as if to a cricket match, the officers with their Fortnum & Mason foods, their silver dressing cases, their valets, coachmen and grooms.

Even in 1914, there was no real understanding of what modern war would be like; everyone thought it would be over in a matter of weeks, and thousands of men queued with alacrity to enlist.

But that was the end. The Conservative party along with the rest of the country emerged from the mud and blood of the First World War determined it should never happen again; and this is the context in which the appeasement policy of the 1930s must be seen. When Neville Chamberlain, in his broadcast of 27th September 1938, said, 'How horrible, fantastic, incredible it is that we should be digging trenches and trying gas masks here because of a quarrel in a faraway country between peoples of whom we know nothing,' he was remembering the wretched suffering of the First World War, and perhaps he was also remembering his father and 'Joe's War' (as people called the Boer War) which began so bravely and ended so badly.

Joe Chamberlain was Colonial Secretary in a Conservative goverment when the long rumbling dispute with the Boers erupted into war in 1899. His part in fomenting it is disputed, but his part in waging it was energetic and enthusiastic. Popular support for 'Joe's War', however, turned to disillusion when the Boers' guerilla tactics began to tell against the mighty British army. To make it worse, all Europe sided with the Boers. Historians liken the effect to the American reaction to the Vietnam conflict. The shock to the British was intense and spurred the speedy moves the Conservative government made away from the 'splendid isolation' of 19th-century foreign policy and towards the international alliances and military build-up that were to play an important part in the 1914–18 war.

Both world wars were waged by nominal coalitions. The first began

Fighting on the north west frontier of India in 1891. Britain and the Conservative party in the 19th century exhibited a complacency born of decades of domestic peace. Lord Salisbury, speaking of frontier wars like these, said, 'They are but the surf which marks the edge and advance of the wave of civilisation.'

Chitral Camp, 1895, when battles in faraway places still looked romantic. Churchill wrote of these distant wars: 'on the frontier, in the clear light of morning, when the mountain side is dotted with smoke puffs, and every ridge sparkles with bright sword blades, the spectator may observe and accurately appreciate all grades of human courage.'

Major-General Sir Bindon Blood (leaning on the gun) and the staff of the Malakand Field Force. Kipling (who was Stanley Baldwin's cousin) chronicled the thoughts of British soldiers fighting for the Empire:

> *Ship me somewheres east of Suez,*
> *where the best is like the worst,*
> *Where there aren't no Ten*
> *Commandments,*
> *an' a man can raise a thirst. . .*

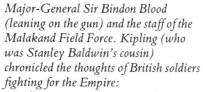

Buller's army finally relieves Ladysmith, 28th February 1900. General Sir George White is on the extreme right. The Boer War was a bitter experience for Britain. Lord Salisbury's military strategy was based on the small battles on the fringe of Empire and was inadequate to the scale of this conflict.

Winston Churchill, First Lord of the Admiralty, with Admiral Fisher in 1914. Churchill's war experience ran the entire gamut from the frontiers of India in the 1890s, the South African plains in 1900, and the active front in the First World War to the corridors of power in both world wars.

A famous naval squadron of the First World War: Vice Admiral Beatty's flagship Lion *leads* Princess Royal, Indomitable *and* New Zealand. *Throughout the 19th century the British navy did indeed rule the waves, but by 1914 the German fleet was a formidable opponent.*

with the Liberals in office under Asquith; but in 1915 he reshuffled his cabinet and brought in some leading Conservatives. In 1916 a convulsion in the Liberal party forced Asquith's resignation, and Lloyd George began his long spectacular reign as Prime Minister. His cabinet, however, was dominated by Conservatives (11 out of 15) and the Tories continued as the major element in the coalition government throughout the war and through the 'coupon election' of 1918. Bonar Law, the Conservative leader, was with Lloyd George at the Peace Conference at Versailles.

In the 1930s, the government was nominally a 'National' coalition again, created this time during the economic crisis of the Labour government in 1931. But the 1931–35 cabinet contained a majority of Conservatives, and the 1935 election returned 432 Conservatives out of a total of 616 MPs; so it was effectively a Conservative government, under the leadership first of Stanley Baldwin and then of Neville Chamberlain.

Much has been written about the failure of this government to prepare Britain for war. Indeed, Stanley Baldwin was so vilified after he left the leadership that when he emerged briefly from a long retirement many years later, frail, aged and rather deaf, the cheers of a small crowd who

Above left *Eerily prescient Dyson cartoon drawn in 1919 shows a 1919 baby (the soldier of 1940) crying as the negotiators leave Versailles. Bonar Law accompanied Lloyd George to the peace conference, and J.C.C. Davidson, then Law's private secretary, later Conservative party Chairman, carried Lloyd George's personal letter concerning the treaty to the King in London.*

Above right *A nursing sister gives sweets to children huddled in an air raid shelter, 1939. The immense collectivising effects of the two great wars were to become a prime concern of post-war Conservative governments. They were still struggling with them three decades later.*

recognised him made him turn to his companion and ask, 'Are they booing me?'

Baldwin and Chamberlain's policy is not intelligible viewed only through the distorting glass of the catastrophe that followed. Europe then had seen ten million soldiers killed in the First World War, another twenty million soldiers and civilians wounded, and £1 billion consumed – 'the accumulated treasure of a century of peace'. Many people who had lived through this would do almost anything to prevent it happening again and would not countenance rearmament, which they saw as preparation for war. Not until 1932 was the 'Ten Year Rule' rescinded, which forced the government to plan defence expenditure on the assumption there would be no great war for at least ten years. Lord Robert Cecil (son of Lord Salisbury, Conservative Prime Minister in the 1890s) was one of those who devoted his entire life to the pursuit of peace, mainly through the League of Nations. He was a prime mover behind the 'Peace Ballot' of 1934–35, in which over eleven million people cast a vote in favour of the League – although their answers were more ambiguous over how to deal with aggression. Throughout the 1930s the Left was a powerful voice against rearmament. The Labour party, just two days after the German coup in the Rhineland, put down an amendment in the Commons that 'this House cannot agree to a policy which seeks security in national armaments'.

Remembering this climate, it is easier to understand why Churchill stood virtually alone in deploring appeasement and urging rearmament. It can almost become a matter of surprise that he was joined at all, and in particular by people like Anthony Eden, who had lost two brothers in the 1914–18 war and had himself been badly wounded. But towards the end of the decade more and more Conservative politicians were associating

January 1940, Neville Chamberlain speaks at the Mansion House during the 'Phoney War'. Disenchantment with him was growing among Conservative MPs, although they (and the majority of the rest of the House of Commons) had endorsed his increasingly desperate search for peace in the 1930s.

The War Cabinet at 10 Downing St., 16th October 1941. Ernest Bevin and Lord Beaverbrook (centre, standing), represented the political extremes Churchill deliberately brought into his government.

Churchill visits Manchester, 29th April 1941. 'Even if all the homes in the country be levelled,' he said, 'then we shall still be found standing together to build them up again after the fighting is over.'

Churchill tours tank units in the Middle East, August 1942.

themselves with Churchill's urgent warnings about the menace of Hitler and the unpreparedness of Britain. It was a matter of desperate controversy, however, and Chamberlain – with the support of the public as well as of most politicians – persevered in his determination to secure 'peace with honour' (a phrase he deliberately echoed from Disraeli's triumphant letter to Queen Victoria following the Congress of Berlin).

After Hitler's contemptuous disregard of the Munich agreement, however, Chamberlain's policy was finished, and Churchill, so ostracised and even ridiculed in the decade of the 1930s, became Prime Minister in May 1940. 'I felt,' he wrote, 'as if I were walking with destiny, and that all my past life had been but a preparation for this hour and for this trial.'

The actual change of leadership was handled in very Conservative style. Chamberlain continued to lead through the months of the 'phoney war', September 1939 to May 1940, but after the failure of the Norwegian campaign, his majority in the House fell from 200 to 80, and he finally resigned as Prime Minister.

The Cabinet, 1979.

Chequers, Buckinghamshire.

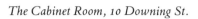

The Cabinet Room, 10 Downing St.

The House of Commons.

There was a slight pause, and some talk of Lord Halifax taking over, but Harold Macmillan (who was watching it all from the back benches) wrote afterwards: 'We needed the nearest thing to Marlborough, to Chatham, or Pitt or Lloyd George. There he was, ready to hand, marked out by destiny – Churchill.'

Churchill as Prime Minister immediately brought into his cabinet people from both ends of the political spectrum, to make a National government: notably Clement Attlee and Ernest Bevin from the left and Lord Beaverbrook from the right. But it was Churchill who waged the war. Lord Blake, in his history of the Conservative party, says: 'the circumstances of war made assets not only of his virtues but of all those defects which had hitherto impeded his political career . . . Now in a desperate struggle for national survival they became positive virtues, along with his courage, tenacity, and a command over language unsurpassed by any previous Prime Minister, equalled by very few.' There is a real question whether the total mobilisation of the country for an effort of unparalleled sacrifice could have been achieved by any lesser figure. One measure of the sacrifice involved are the figures on personal expenditure: in 1941 spending on food was 20% *less* than in 1938, on household goods 43% less, on clothing 38% less, on private motoring 76% less. A more horrific measure is the numbers the war killed: 17 million soldiers dead, 43 million civilians. At the height of the Battle of Britain, which Hitler saw as preliminary to his actual invasion, more than 9000 tons of bombs were dropped in a single month on the cities and towns of England.

Through it all Churchill dominated – not only the military effort, but the civilian scene as well. His speeches to the House were reported everywhere by radio. On 5th June 1940 Vita Sackville West heard one and wrote her husband: 'Even repeated by the announcer it sent shivers (not of fear) down my spine.' The speech she had just heard included this famous passage: 'We shall not flag or fail. We shall fight in France, we shall fight on the seas and oceans, we shall fight with growing confidence and growing strength in the air, we shall defend our island, whatever the cost may be, we shall fight on the beaches, we shall fight on the landing grounds, we shall fight in the fields and in the streets, we shall fight in the hills; we shall never surrender.'

The three-plus decades since the end of the war have blurred the outlines of its magnitude, but its impact shaped all the years thereafter. The American writer Herbert Agar, who was Special Assistant to the US

Anthony Eden, with gasmask, walks to his wartime office in Whitehall. Chamberlain forced Eden's resignation as Foreign Secretary in 1938 and replaced him with Viscount Halifax. It startled Tory MPs and fed their growing disillusionment with Chamberlain's leadership.

VE Day. Churchill waves to jubilant crowds outside Parliament.

REARMAMENT

"IT'S SO HORRIBLY DANGEROUS!"

"WELL THERE'S ALWAYS THIS ALTERNATIVE"..

Ambassador in London from 1942 to 1946, wrote: 'Maybe the tyrant state will prove to be the "wave of the future". Man may find himself too harassed by his own inventions to take the trouble to remain free. This catastrophe, if it is fated, has now been postponed for several generations. We have been given another chance, and we have been given it by the people of Great Britain. I would find it churlish if we were to forget this, and not even say thank you.'

This passage touches upon the side effects of the two world wars that especially concern the Conservative party: no such gigantic conflicts could

Above left *Winston Churchill, MP for Epping, warns Britain in 1933 of the growing military might of Germany.*

Above right *Winston Churchill, MP for Stretford, warns Britain in 1977 of the growing military might of the Soviet Union.*

be successfully waged and won without massive collectivisation and regimentation of the civilian population. The process was apparent in the first and even more so in the second. For instance, the Emergency Powers Act of May 1940 decreed that the Minister of Labour (who in 1940 was Ernest Bevin) could direct any person in the UK to perform any service anywhere; he could prescribe remuneration and conditions of work and impose administrative requirements on workers and employers alike. The National Service Act of December 1941 required all persons between the ages of 18 and 60 to perform some kind of national service. Rationing, wage and price control and an enormous increase in government expenditure were all part of the war effort. No one disputed (then or now) that these measures were necessary in the desperate circumstances of the time, but their effect unquestionably was to accustom people to a degree of government control and interference that in peacetime they never would have tolerated. Also, the strong central direction that gave such impetus to war production encouraged an enthusiasm for unobstructed central planning in peacetime. Both the size of government and the power of central planners were endorsed and in some respects extended by the Labour government of 1945–51. As the Conservative party is opposed both to excessive government control and to unfettered central planning, its policy when it returned to office in 1951 (and subsequently) was to reduce both.

If the experience of the First World War caused the party to recoil from the mere idea of war, the experience of the Second taught them more realistic ways to prevent it. Alec Douglas-Home when he was in India in 1955, explained to the Council of Foreign Affairs the substance of the Conservative policy after the war: 'Three times in half a century we held out the olive branch of conciliation to the Kaiser, to Hitler and to Stalin, and the lessons we and our friends in Europe have learned in a bitter

Margaret Thatcher flew to Northern Ireland, 29th August 1979, immediately following the IRA murder of Lord Mountbatten, to demonstate the government's determination to resist terrorist pressure. There continues to be all-party agreement on policy towards the conflict in Northern Ireland.

school is that weakness invites aggression and that neutrality has no meaning in the context of totalitarian ambition.'

From this platform the Conservative party has given consistent support to NATO and to the maintenance of defence expenditure. Today they see Communism as the current pursuer of 'totalitarian ambition'. Reginald Maudling, Conservative shadow Foreign Secretary in 1976, said, 'The Conservative Party has one overriding concern in foreign policy, and that is the growth of Communist power and influence in the world, and the dangers it can bring for all of us.' When Margaret Thatcher repeated Conservative concern at the expansion of Soviet Communist power in a series of speeches in 1976, she was attacked violently in Russian newspapers, which said her speeches were 'provocative' and called her 'the Iron Lady'. It was the kind of attack Winston Churchill would have recognised.

CHAPTER 11
The Workers

IN 1952, just after the Conservatives had won the first, as it turned out, of three consecutive election victories, the Labour party published a disheartened and disbelieving pamphlet. In it, the author, Peter Shore, said: 'Once the mass of the people had the vote, Socialists were convinced that Conservatism and all that it stood for would be swept away. Their victory seemed certain, for Conservatism which was based on privilege and wealth was inevitably a minority creed, whereas Socialism, with its appeal to social justice and economic self-interest, would recruit the big battalions of the poor and unprivileged . . . Yet it is clear that events have falsified these predictions . . . The question which must now be asked is why the fruits of universal suffrage have taken so long to ripen.'

The Conservative answer is that the fruits of universal suffrage have indeed ripened – it is just that they are the fruits the voters wanted, not the ones the early socialists expected. The reason it happened goes a long way toward explaining why the Tories have gained ground, not lost it, in the years of mass suffrage: the new voters wanted not to eliminate privilege and wealth, but to share it.

And they have: the unenfranchised property-less uneducated 'big battalions' the socialists expected to turn to revolution have turned instead into a populace where everyone is educated to at least the age of 16, where every British adult (save lunatics, Lords and prisoners) has a vote, where everyone has access to health care, old age pensions, unemployment benefit and poverty relief, where over 96% of households have television sets, 87% have refrigerators, over half own cars, and 99% of full time workers have three or more weeks paid holiday a year.

This profound revolution in the lives of ordinary people happened during a period when the Tories were in office almost two-thirds of the

Engraving from 1842 purports to show Shaftesbury inspecting child labour in the mines. Shaftesbury's Royal Commission Report, illustrated with pictures like this, shocked the nation, and his speech in the House was so powerful, it is reported, that MPs wept. The Report led to Peel's government passing laws against women and children working in the mines.

Above left *Membership certificate from 1864 of the 'General Union of House Carpenters and Joiners'. It was a Tory government in 1824 that made trade unions legal by repealing the repressive Combination Acts, and Disraeli in 1875 who reinstated the right of peaceful picketing.*

Above right *One of the oldest Conservative Working Men's Clubs in the country: the Croydon Club moved into this building in January 1888; in 1968 they moved into one three times the size, with 2 bars, billiard room, concert room, children's room, darts, dances and weekly cabaret. The working men's clubs, with their mix of politics and socialising, were an important factor in the Tories' continued success as the electorate enlarged.*

time, a period – Robert McKenzie points out in a classic study of working class Conservatives – when 'the Conservatives have had a record of success almost unrivalled among political parties in parliamentary systems.'

The enormity of this British revolution is often ignored in the heat and clash of contemporary strife; so is the fact that the contemporary strife itself is being fought on the grounds 'we want more', not 'we want to sweep it all away.'

The noise and dust of contemporary strife has also obscured something even more important: the question Robert McKenzie asks in his book and Peter Shore in his pamphlet – i.e. 'Why do workers vote Conservative?' – is revealing of a longstanding confusion in 20th-century British politics: the idea that British political parties are organised along 'class warfare' lines. Workers, and laws to safeguard them and to legalise their unions, all existed long before the birth of the Labour party in 1900. The Tories made trade unions legal by repealing the Combination Acts in 1824; Peel's Conservative government passed the act that set the precedent for stopping industrial exploitation; Disraeli passed the Factory Acts and extended the franchise to working class householders. It was the Conservatives who passed the first act for workmen's compensation and set up the first unemployment committees. Throughout the 19th century the Conservatives battled the laissez-faire Liberals for legislation on behalf of workers. It was Conservative Working Men's Associations and Clubs that joined together to form the National Union in 1867. This is not the record of a group antagonistic to the interests of working people.

The confusion began with the birth of the Labour party and is a result of the special circumstances of that birth: the Labour party is descended directly from the Parliamentary Committee of the Trades Union Congress. The Trades Union Congress (TUC) began in 1868, and its Parliamentary Committee, set up in 1871 to lobby MPs on behalf of trade unions, was an important influence on the labour legislation passed in the 1870s.

However, in 1900, some members decided simply lobbying was not enough, and so, under the aegis of the TUC they formed the Labour Representation Committee specifically to sponsor candidates – financially

(C.C.O.—July, 1895.—No. 262)

FREEDOM for WORKING MEN

What Trade Unions owe to the Conservatives

The Conservative Party are accused at present of being enemies of Trade Unionism. This charge is absolutely false. It is true that Conservatives are opposed to the coercive policy of modern Trade Unions, which denies freedom of contract to the workman in cases even where he has everything to gain; but it is largely due to the Conservative Party that Trade Unionism owes its very existence.

Up to 1824 Unions among workmen were entirely forbidden, and although from that date both parties had a share in securing the **right of combination**, it is certain that this as well as many other of the advantages that working men now enjoy are due to the action of Conservative Statesmen.

The **Combination Laws**, a series of mediæval statutes forbidding workmen to join together for almost any common purpose, were repealed in 1824, under the strong Tory Government then in power. In 1825 the same Ministry passed an Act by which combinations for regulating the rate of wages and the hours of work were expressly exempted from the law against "conspiracy," and under this Act, which remained unaltered for nearly forty years, **Trade Unions** sprang up in large numbers throughout the country.

Conservative Statesmen, in 1855, secured for Trades Unions the advantages enjoyed by **Friendly Societies**. In 1859 the late Lord Derby's Conservative Government passed an Act further extending the liberty of combination, and in 1868 a Conservative Member, Mr. Russell Gurney, carried a measure for the protection of Trade Union Funds.

and electorally – for Parliament. This Committee was renamed the Labour party in 1906. It was perfectly straightforward: the Labour party represented the trade unions. Not the 'workers' – total membership of the TUC was 2 to 4 million before the First World War, while the number of people employed – working – numbered 16 to 18 million. (In 1978, out of a workforce of about 26 million and a population of 55 million, about 12 million were members of unions.)

Given the adversary nature of British politics – symbolised by the design of the House of Commons – it was inevitable that if one party announced it was 'for' the unions, the assumption would be the other was 'against'. As the Labour party grew and ousted the Liberals as the second major party in the state, it was politically advantageous to expand the idea of representing 'unions' into representing 'workers' and to present themselves as 'pro' and Tories as 'anti'.

The Conservatives have not, of course, been blameless in the creation of this image. For instance, the Taff Vale decision, in 1901, which awarded damages against a union for supporting a strike, was upheld by the Tory-dominated House of Lords and appeared to many to contradict the Conservative legislation on unions passed in the 1870s. This decision unquestionably spurred the growth of militant union feeling (membership of the Labour Representation Committee leaped from 356,000 to 861,000, and they began to win by-elections). Taff Vale was also an important cause of the Trade Disputes Act of 1906 which made unions immune from liability in tort – a position they still hold.

Probably more than any other event, the 1926 General Strike contributed to the 'pro' and 'anti' images of the Labour and Conservative parties. A Conservative government was in power; the TUC called the strike. The TUC was not only sponsoring the Labour MPs; it shared its building with the party (and continued to do so until 1958 when the TUC moved, but the party continued to share the headquarters of the Transport and General Workers Union). The Labour party therefore was inextricably linked with the TUC, the Tories with everyone else. For nine days in May 1926 two sections of the country faced each other across battle lines clearly drawn. The heated and sometimes lurid rhetoric was heavily influenced by the recent revolution in Russia and by the aggressive calls to

Above left Handbill from the election of July 1895. Despite mythology to the contrary, it has been workers and trade unionists who have kept the Conservative party in power for more years than any other. Given the composition of the electorate, the Tories have to draw at least half their support from the 'workers' in order to win. See also the modern poster on page 138.

Above right General Election, December 1910: the Conservative candidate for Newton (Lord Wolmer) goes down the old Boston pit in Haydock to deliver a speech to the miners. The contemporary caption (from the Illustrated London News) states: 'The visit, which was a surprise one, was very popular and terminated only when Lord Wolmer had made a tour of the pit.'

Opposite page below 'The Derby 1867': Disraeli pipped the other would-be reformers at the post with his Act of 1867 which enfranchised working men. The electorate was virtually doubled, with the new voters coming mainly from the urban working classes.

Above left *General Strike, 1926: a flood of volunteers poured in to man essential services. Here one drives a bus, protected by a policeman. Note barbed wire on the bonnet.*

Above right *Strikers marching down Park Lane, May 1926. There was widespread fear among the middle classes that the Strike might be part of a Communist plot (understandably, with banners like this on Park Lane). This fear partly underlay pressure for the Conservatives to pass the ill-advised Trade Union Act (1927) which was repealed in 1946.*

Centre right *The General Strike, May 1926: Neville Chamberlain and Leo Amery leave 10 Downing St. on 'Crisis Sunday'. This direct confrontation between a Conservative government and the TUC has coloured relations ever since. A measure of the changes the years have brought, however, is to remember that the spark that ignited the General Strike was the mine owners' proposal to actually lower miners' wages and lengthen their hours of work.*

Below right *The shipbuilding yard at Jarrow closed in 1936, and the workers marched to London to publicise their need for help. Although there were pockets of severe unemployment and hardship, concentrated in the areas of old decaying industries, living standards as a whole actually rose during the 1930s.*

Winston Churchill edited the government's newsheet during the strike. It may have leant more towards inflaming than informing, but it was widely read. This is the edition of 12th May, the day the TUC called off the strike.

extend it by Zinoviev, the President of the Communist International. Foreigners and historians have congratulated all parties that violent revolution was averted in 1926, but the confrontation passed into folk-mythology and was not forgotten.

The Conservatives have been unable to shake this legacy in all the intervening years, despite the fact that in every election this century at least half their votes have come from the sociologically categorised 'working class'.

This image may or may not have electorally harmed the Tory party (it has won more often this century than it has lost), but historically more important is the assumption, implicit in this image, of 'class warfare'. The dangers as well as the error of this assumption are a theme that has been stressed repeatedly by Conservative politicians: by denying the essential homogeneity and unity of interests of modern British society, they say, this idea of warring classes draws a red herring across the track that might otherwise be followed toward increased national prosperity.

Stanley Baldwin, persuading his own party not to pass a contentious piece of trade union legislation in 1924, made his famous 'Peace in Industry' speech on this theme (which in pamphlet form sold half a

David Low in the Evening Standard, *July 1928, succinctly states the problem that defeated politicians between the wars. Neither Baldwin nor MacDonald could make an impression on the intractable lump of unemployment.*

Candles are lit to read the bad news in February 1972. Industrial disputes were a constant feature throughout the 1970s under both Labour and Conservative governments, following the failure of either to implement reforms of trade union law.

million copies in three months): 'We, at any rate,' he said, 'are not going to fire the first shot. We stand for peace. We stand for the removal of suspicion in the country. We want to create an atmosphere, a new atmosphere in a new Parliament for a new age, in which the people can come together.'

R.A. Butler, charged after the Second World War with reshaping the Conservative party's intellectual base, emphasised this theme again in the Industrial Charter, which had as one of its major objects 'the need to strengthen by example and precept the channels of communication and cooperation between management and workers. Very often major labour difficulties had been avoided by the interest and enthusiasm of top company executives, who had broken away from the idea of industry being divided into two sides and helped to promote a new spirit of involvement and satisfaction through joint consultation, works committees and co-partnership schemes.'

However, despite the aims repeatedly stated in party manifestos and in politicians' speeches, relations with the unions continued to be a problem – and not only for the Tories. Every year since the war, no matter which party was in power, there were well over a thousand strikes and work stoppages, and most years saw over two thousand. In 1965 the then Labour government set up a Royal Commission on Trades Unions and Employers Associations under Lord Donovan which reported in 1968. Following this the Labour government published proposals for trade union reform in a white paper entitled *In Place of Strife* (1969). It encountered fierce opposition from the unions and was not enacted into law.

The Conservative government under Edward Heath passed the Industrial Relations Act in 1971, which followed closely the recommendations of the Donovan Commission, and also incorporated many of the proposals of *In Place of Strife*. This Act also ran into fierce opposition from some sections of organised labour and was rendered ineffective by the non-cooperation of the major unions.

It was in the 1970s that all the birds came home to roost, for both parties. For the Conservatives the inherited legacy of being 'anti union' exacerbated the conflicts in 1970–74 caused by economic difficulties. For the Labour party the unbreakable bonds that linked them with the unions made it impossible for them to control the industrial situation when they returned to power in 1974. The distinguished left-wing writer Hugh Thomas, who was a Labour Parliamentary candidate, left the Labour party and joined the Tories in the middle 1970s. Concerning this issue he said, 'I hoped the Labour party could cut itself free from the trade unions and mature into something comparable to the Democratic Party in the US. That never happened, and certainly looks unlikely now.'

The February 1974 election was fought – by force of circumstance – on the question of union power. The particular issue that forced the election, well in advance of the timing the Tories would have chosen, was the National Union of Mineworkers' demand for a pay rise substantially in excess of Phase Three of the Heath government's pay policy. The miners backed their demand with a ban on overtime that threatened to cut production some 30%. This, coupled with the oil crisis brought on by the Arab–Israeli war and an electricians' overtime ban, caused the government to order a three-day working week to start in January 1974 and (even more damaging according to some observers) stopped all television broadcasting at 10.30 every night.

The miners voted (81% in favour) for an all-out strike early in

February 1979: a cancer patient at Westminster Hospital learns his operation has been postponed yet again due to a strike by hospital workers. The industrial disruption in the winter of 1978–79 under a Labour government was thought by many to have been a factor in the Conservative win in May.

1st February 1974: miners at the Snowdown Colliery in Kent exhibit their ballot cards for the pithead vote on whether or not to strike. 81% voted 'Yes' and it precipitated the election of 28th February. In December 1979 the miners voted 'No' to a strike call.

137

WHY EVERY TRADE UNIONIST SHOULD CONSIDER VOTING CONSERVATIVE.

The Labour Party likes to see itself as the party of the working man.

That's how Labour has established such close links with the Trade Unions.

And there's no doubt that there was a time when the Labour Party made real efforts to improve conditions for workers in this country.

But what good have these close ties done the average working man in recent years?

WHAT LABOUR HAS DONE FOR THE WORKING MAN SINCE THE WAR.

Since 1945, both parties have had roughly the same number of years in power.

In over 16 years of Labour government take home pay of the average industrial worker has gone up, in real terms, by 6%.

In the same period of Conservative government take home pay of the average industrial worker has gone up, in real terms, by 60%.

You don't need a computer to see that the average worker has been 10 times better off with the Conservatives.

HAVE THE CONSERVATIVES JUST BEEN LUCKY?

How have the Conservatives managed to do so much more for the working man?

The fact is you can't increase real wages without increasing production.

And Labour haven't managed to get production moving.

Since the war, in the 16 years under Labour, production only went up *half as much* as it did with the Conservative governments. That's why real wages under Labour haven't grown as fast.

Low production means low wages.

High production means high wages.

Frankly, Labour just don't seem to understand how to get production moving. They don't know how to motivate firms to take on more people.

They don't know how to create a climate in which firms can afford to pay people more and produce more.

The key to higher production isn't government hand-outs and subsidies. It's greater incentives to companies and people.

THE LAST 4 YEARS SEEM TO PROVE THE POINT.

In the last few years, the living standards of workers in this country have been badly hit. The Labour government's explanation for this is that Britain has been suffering because the whole world has been suffering.

Well, the fact is that the world did have a bit of a cold ... but it seems to be getting over the worst of it. In Britain that cold seems to have turned into double pneumonia.

Look at France. Between 1974-1977 the average French worker saw his wages, in terms of what they'll buy, go up by over 18%.

In Germany, the average worker saw his real wages go up by 12%.

The average Dutch worker saw his real wages go up by over 11%.

Meanwhile, in Britain, the average industrial worker saw his real wages, in terms of what they will buy, actually go down.

And it isn't just the French, Germans and Dutch who have done better. The British worker has also done worse than, for example, workers in Thailand, S. Korea, Spain, Portugal, Greece, etc.

WHY HAVE BRITAIN'S WORKERS SUFFERED SO BADLY?

In the last four years in Britain, manufacturing production has actually *fallen*. So real wages couldn't grow. Without any growth in production, Labour have had to have one round of wage control after another ...first £6, then £4, then 10%, now down to 5%.

Now if you produce less, you're restricted on what you can earn, and therefore you're also restricted on what you can buy. If you have to buy less, someone else will have to make less, and that's why today there are so many members of British trade unions not making anything. They're out of work.

The tragic truth is that since Labour came to power, another person has joined the unemployment queue every 3 minutes.

This Labour government, the party whose advertising slogan was "Back to work with Labour," has presided over unemployment levels unseen in this country for decades.

Now the amazing thing is this.

Every Labour government since the war has left more people unemployed when it left office than when it came into office.

WHAT'S LABOUR'S PROBLEM?

It is not that Labour don't want to get production and wages rising. Of course they do. It's not that they don't care about the unemployed. Labour's real problem is their basic philosophy.

They still seem to be fighting the class war that Karl Marx saw in the last century.

The Labour Party is still clinging on to the idea of redistributing wealth.

But what is the use of redistributing wealth when the country has very little wealth to redistribute?

For example, if no one was allowed to keep more than £10,000 of their earnings after tax, the rest of us wouldn't even get enough to buy a box of paper tissues every week.

In fact, their idealistic philosophy actually makes things worse. This philosophy makes the people who want to get the best for themselves and their family feel guilty – and the rest envious if they succeed.

The Labour philosophy taxes ambition, enthusiasm, achievement, the very things that create wealth. That's why, as the facts on record show, Labour's aim of redistributing wealth ends up as distributing poverty.

THE TRADE UNIONS & SOCIAL SERVICES.

The Trade Union movement has often fought for better standards of social services; better schools, housing, hospitals, care for the elderly and under-privileged.

The Labour Party has always expressed to the Trade Unions that it has the best intentions in these areas. Sadly, as the past four years have shown, you can't pay for better social services with good intentions. Caring that works costs cash.

It all seems to come down to one thing. Money – and the policies which create it. Labour never seem to have enough. Strange, you might think, when we're paying more tax under this present Labour government than ever before.

But despite all this tax they're collecting, they still haven't got enough to pay for the proper standards of social services. And they never can get enough coming in from tax, when people aren't earning and producing enough in the first place.

We all know with Labour's production record, people can't earn enough. So the Labour government has to take more and more of what they do earn to try and pay for the schools, hospitals and social services we all want.

This is not opinion. It is the official government record:

Since the war every Labour government has increased income tax.

And every Conservative government has cut income tax.

Yet every Conservative government since the war has been able to increase the amount spent on social services.

How is this possible? As we've seen since the war, with the Conservatives real earnings rose by ten times more than under Labour.

So Conservative governments could afford to take a smaller share of your earnings in tax and still be left with enough in the kitty to pay for the proper standards of social services we all want.

SHOULD YOU BE VOTING CONSERVATIVE?

In fact, it is reckoned that up to one out of every three Trade Unionist voters now vote Conservative.

Even so, some Trade Unionists may still feel traditionally tied to the Labour Party, and might find it strange to vote Conservative.

To them the Conservative Party makes this promise.

The next Conservative government will concentrate all its efforts to break out of this depressing cycle of low production and low wages – and restore the system of responsible and realistic pay bargaining, free from government interference.

Freedom from government interference has always been a traditional principle of the Trade Union movement – and freedom from government interference is also a traditional principle of the Conservative Party.

Even if you're a lifetime Labour voter, please vote in the coming election on the *actual record* of the two parties.

Because that record seems to prove conclusively that the Conservatives, in trying to look after the nation as a whole, do a better job of looking after the working man than the so-called working man's party.

THE CONSERVATIVE PARTY

A poster from the election of May 1979 continues an old tradition: see the 1895 handbill on page 133.

February, and the election was almost immediately called for the 28th. Thus circumstances forced the election to be fought on the issue 'Who governs?' – but the result did not answer the question. There was no clear winner: the Conservatives had 37.8% of the vote, Labour 37.1%. Parliamentary seats were 297 Conservative, 301 Labour, 14 Liberal, 23 others. It was all re-run again in October 1974 and Labour won a Parliamentary majority of 3 over all other parties.

From 1974 the Tories made a systematic effort to clarify their position with regard to trade unions. Jim Prior, the Conservative Secretary of State for Employment under Mrs Thatcher, said while in opposition: 'We shall encourage people to join unions, but we shall guard the legitimate interests of those who don't . . . We shall seek the maximum cooperation and consult fully, but governments are entrusted by the people to govern, and no group can be allowed to take away that responsibility.'

The party also made a determined effort to identify and encourage their supporters within the trade union movement, primarily through the development of the Conservative Trade Unionist organisation (CTU), which they built from 50 member groups in 1975 to 280 in 1978.

The winter of 1979, immediately preceding the General Election, was one of intense industrial strife. Hospitals closed, schools closed, corpses were unburied and rubbish uncollected. Road haulage was severely curtailed, there was violence on picket lines, and the Labour government's 5% pay guideline was overwhelmed by wage demands five and six times the size. In the post-mortem following the election, Tory and Labour supporters alike pointed to the record in the winter as an important factor in the Conservative victory.

CHAPTER 12
The Economy

THE 'ECONOMY' did not exist in the 19th century – at least not in the sense we know it, a gigantic interlinked mechanism 'managed' by the government and affecting everyone in every aspect of their lives. The idea that their governments might control and regulate the entire economic life of the country would have appalled Peel and made Disraeli laugh.

Not that they were unaware of economic forces operating in a modern state, nor of some of the ways government might affect them; but thinking about 'political economy' (as they called it) in the 19th century was very much conditioned by the ideas of Adam Smith contained in his book *An Inquiry into the Nature and Causes of the Wealth of Nations* (said by the *Encyclopedia Britannica* to be 'a work in which wisdom, learning and the power of analysis are joined to an extraordinary degree'). Even if the politicians of the day had not actually read it, Adam Smith's ideas, at once simple and profound, had sunk deep into the minds of political decision makers, just as the ideas of John Maynard Keynes were to do in the middle of the 20th century.

Adam Smith believed (among other things) in free trade between individuals and between nations; he believed that every man (and every country) pursuing his own interests in his own way was far more likely to benefit society as a whole than monopolies, restrictive practices, controls or protective tariffs. In stating this, he marked out the battlefield on which politicians, and in particular Conservative politicians, were to fight throughout the 19th century.

They fought over the Corn Laws and over all the tariffs descended from them, which had as their object the protection of domestic interests, whether landed or industrial. It was the effects of these tariffs, in keeping prices up and in restricting the free interchange of goods, that were the sources of the conflict. In 1846 Peel repealed the Corn Law tariff, in the interests of free trade. It was an action for which he gained the adulation of the people and the enmity of the landed interests of his party, who withdrew their support as the result of his 'betrayal' and split the party

A £5 note from one of the more than 400 private banks entitled to issue paper money before Peel's Bank Charter Act (1844) which gave a monopoly of issue in England and Wales to the Bank of England (although the last private note did not stop circulating until 1921). Peel's fiscal measures were the foundation of Victorian prosperity.

Right *Peel introduced the first peacetime income tax in 1842 at 7d in the pound (less than 3%). It was as unpopular then as now, but it was this idea of a graduated tax – practical, predictable and equitable – that allowed the Victorians their free trade policies and their spectacular expansion of state services.*

A DIP IN THE FREE TRADE SEA.

"THERE, TAKE OFF HIS COAT LIKE A GOOD LITTLE BEN, AND COME TO HIS COBDEN."

Above *A dubious Disraeli is encouraged by the famous free trader Richard Cobden to take the plunge and support the bracing competitive climate of free trade. He did in fact change his stand from protectionist to free trader. A belief in the invigorating effects of competition is a consistent strand in Conservative economic thought.*

Right *The jubilant Free Trade Hat commemorated repeal of the Corn Laws. For 100 years the most burning economic question was free trade v. protection. It split the Conservative party at least three times. Today the major economic arguments revolve around unemployment and pay. It reflects a shift in emphasis from concern with the creation of wealth to concern with its distribution.*

irreconcilably in half. Peel saw his action (he told the House of Commons) as easing the lives of 'those whose lot it is to labour' by providing for 'abundant and untaxed food'. Disraeli said that Peel, by removing protection for British agriculture, had acted like a nurse who 'dashed out the brains' of the baby in her care.

At the end of the century this same issue – free trade *v.* tariffs – divided the party yet again. Joe Chamberlain, the radical populist who was the Tories' uneasy ally after 1886, led the 'tariff reformers' who saw import

The opening of the Eastern Union Railway, 1846; in this year 272 railway companies were sanctioned by Parliament. The railways had a profound effect on Victorian society – accelerating the expansion of industry and giving poor people mobility for the first time. They were wholly a result of private enterprise; given the attitudes of the time, government was not involved at all in their development.

The interior of the Stock Exchange, 1847, sketched (according to the contemporary caption) 'during one of the days of the great Money Panic'. 1847–48 was a period of slump, and economic depression (then as now) fuelled discontent even as affluence defused it. The Chartist movement grew apace, and Tories wondered if the Continental revolutions would spread to England.

1859: Lord Derby as PM is lobbied on the subject of the paper duty. The government was facing growing expenditure demands – in 1859 notably the necessary refurbishing of the Navy – and was concerned for its revenue.

taxes as the way to protect domestic industry, foster Empire unity and retaliate against the tariffs other countries had imposed. But most of the Conservative party was deeply and emotionally attached to free trade and would not have tariffs at any price. The party split and was out of power for a decade.

Besides free trade, Adam Smith also believed in the state establishing institutions and public works for the benefit of society as a whole, if they were 'of such a nature that the profit could never repay the expense to any

Huntley & Palmer's biscuit factory, 1882. As industry became mechanised more and more products were produced at less and less cost. To Victorian industrialists it seemed an economic miracle indeed. The political problem was to persuade them that humane conditions were not incompatible with profits.

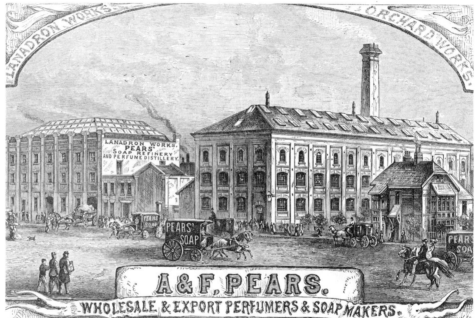

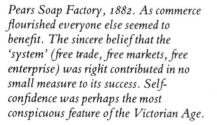

Pears Soap Factory, 1882. As commerce flourished everyone else seemed to benefit. The sincere belief that the 'system' (free trade, free markets, free enterprise) was right contributed in no small measure to its success. Self-confidence was perhaps the most conspicuous feature of the Victorian Age.

individual or small number of individuals'. To pay for such activities he recommended a proportionate tax: 'it is not very unreasonable that the rich should contribute to the public expense, not only in proportion to their revenue, but something more than in that proportion.' Peel agreed with him, and instituted the first peacetime income tax in 1842, which he used to eliminate the government's deficit and to make sweeping reductions in existing tariffs. These measures had the effect of reducing the cost of living and, according to historians, were important factors in damping down unrest and preventing the Continental revolutions of the 1840s from spreading to England.

Peel was also a great believer in sound money – money firmly backed by gold bullion stacked in the vaults of the Bank of England. He had been witness to the wild inflation that had accompanied the Napoleonic Wars when Britain came off the Gold Standard in 1797, and he was chairman of the currency committee of 1819 that recommended a return to it. As Prime Minister in 1841–46 he determinedly pursued a policy of 'sound money', tying the Bank of England's issue of paper notes firmly to its supply of gold, and beginning the long process of ending the issue of

The Conservative Conference, 1979.

*Heath's first garden party at 10
Downing St. in 1970.*

Counting the votes at the 1979 election.

The State Opening of Parliament.

High St., Reading, with the new motors, at the beginning of this century. Average real incomes rose by nearly a third in the years 1880–1900. Peel appeared to have been right when he said in 1844: 'General prosperity, and not legal enactments, produce a practical effect upon the rate of wages.'

notes by private banks (although the last one did not stop until 1921).

These and Peel's other fiscal reforms are credited with creating the framework which enabled the Victorian economy to expand so spectacularly. Throughout the 19th century London was the financial capital of the world, her banks rock-solid, her currency even more so. Industry expanded at home, investments multiplied abroad and everyone got richer. From a base line of 100 in 1850, average wages rose to 156 by 1874 and did not subsequently drop below 148 despite the agricultural slumps. Streets were meanwhile being paved and lighted, slums were being cleared, public water, sanitation, transport and mass education were being provided. British exports in 1842 were valued at £47 million: by 1870 they were £200 million. 'The tide of material progress,' said the historian R.C.K. Ensor, 'flowed up all sorts of creeks and inlets. Here is one illustration: the National Gallery, founded in 1824, increased the number of its pictures between 1870 and 1890 by 50 per cent.'

Right to the end of the century Britain's condition was prosperous and continuously improving. No wonder the 19th century had such confidence in the ideas of Adam Smith. All their experience seemed directly to vindicate a belief in free enterprise, in competition and in the ineluctable rewards of labour and capital earnestly invested.

But in the 20th century things changed. For one thing, the evils so visible in the exercise of unrestricted free enterprise demanded government action (see page 95). This in itself was not contrary to the ideas of Adam Smith ('those exertions of the natural liberty of a few individuals which might endanger the security of the whole society are, and ought to be, restrained by the laws of all governments'). But it foreshadowed the major phenomenon of 20th-century Britain – the gigantic growth in the activity of the state.

Another reason things changed was the inexorable growth in the complexity of the country's affairs. The economic issues of the 19th century – free trade, progressive taxation, the operation and role of banks – which could be readily understood by MPs and their electorates, passed in the 20th century into realms of such intricacy that ordinary people had no hope of following. The debate began to be conducted with increased heat and in incomprehensible language – 'general equilibrium analysis', 'marginal utility theory'. And it was not just the electorate who did not understand the new language. When Churchill, as Chancellor of the

Budget Day, 1928: Winston Churchill as Chancellor of the Exchequer leaves Downing St. for Parliament with Robert (later Lord) Boothby. Churchill's period as Chancellor is chiefly remembered for the return to the gold standard in 1925, a move enthusiastically supported by the Treasury and the Bank of England, but based on Victorian ideas of 'sound money' and inappropriate to the needs of the 20th century.

John Maynard Keynes, the most influential economist of the 20th century. His impact on Conservative policy was profound. During the war he was an adviser to the Treasury, and after the war his ideas on government's role in managing the economy influenced successive Conservative administrations.

Exchequer in 1925, was faced with the question whether to return to the Gold Standard (which had been suspended during the First World War after a century of unbroken adherence) his decision to return to it (savagely criticised later) was complicated by the warring views of economic advisors, and he was doubtless more influenced by his historian's knowledge of the prosperity of the Victorian age. 'I pass with relief,' he once said in another context, 'from the tossing sea of Cause and Theory to the firm ground of Result and Fact.'

This was the position of most Conservative – and indeed Liberal and Labour – politicians in the 1920s and 1930s. The seeming certainties of Victorian economic policy turned to quicksand in the conditions of intractable unemployment and depression with which they now were faced. The decisions they took, lacking any consistent theoretical base, were empirical, not doctrinaire. Stanley Baldwin, for instance, the Conservative Prime Minister through most of the 1920s and 1930s, created some of the first nationalised industries: the BBC and the Central Electricity Generating Board. But in the serious slump of the 1930s, when unemployed reached over two and a half million under the short-lived Labour administration of 1929–31, Conservative politicians as well as Labour and Liberal were unclear what to do. Most Conservatives decided that financial orthodoxy – 'sound money' – was the only possible salvation. The idea that what had worked before must work again led them to cling to the Gold Standard and to a balanced budget, which in turn required reduced government expenditure, reduced wages in the state sector and support for wage reductions in the private sector.

Into this situation of confusion and misunderstanding came John Maynard Keynes, a brilliant Cambridge don who had been the chief

British Treasury representative at the peace negotiations at Versailles, and who had correctly forecast the disastrous economic results of the treaty. Much of what he wrote in his influential book *The General Theory of Employment, Interest and Money* (1936) was not altogether new, but its immense impact was due at least in part to the fact he said it in language that could be understood. Out of the impenetrable mists of 'monopsony' and 'liquidity preference analysis' came the clear proposition that when there was not enough demand for goods, production slumped and recession and unemployment followed; when there was too much demand for goods, prices went up and inflation was the result.

This satisfying intelligible explanation of problems previously inexplicable to many led inevitably to the idea that it was possible to control demand by using government policy as a managing tool; i.e. in an inflationary period the government could reduce demand by raising taxes, reducing the supply of money and cutting government expenditure. In periods of unemployment the process could be reversed.

Keynes' influence on Conservative politicians went well beyond his writings. He was invited to join Churchill's wartime government as an advisor to the Treasury and played a key role in the financing of the war, and in the discussion of how to tackle post-war problems. The idea, for instance, that serious depression was inevitable if post-war government expenditure did not match wartime spending (disproved by the tremendous drop in US government spending which did not result in depression) was traceable to Keynes.

To understand the impact Keynes had on Conservative (as well as other) politicians one has to realise how very badly they wished to end the recurring evils of depression and unemployment, and how desperately

First meeting of the Cabinet of the 'National Government' at Downing St., 1931. Ramsay MacDonald and his Labour government were unable to cope with the economic crisis of 1929, and in August 1931 MacDonald asked the Conservatives and Liberals to join a coalition. In the picture, MacDonald is the first in line, Baldwin fourth, Chamberlain seventh.

The British Housewives League stage a demonstration at the House of Commons in April 1951 to protest at the economic situation. The prolonging of wartime shortages and controls was an important factor in the Conservative election win in October 1951. A campaign slogan was 'Set the people free!'

July 1954: rationing ends at last after 14 years, and a delighted 'mother of 6, grandmother of 10' tears up her book. During the years of Conservative administrations, 1951–64, living standards rose over 60%. Increasing affluence (as before) defused discontent, and (as before) there was naive expectation it would last for ever.

they wanted to avoid a repetition of the 1930s. Harold Macmillan was one of those deeply marked by the experiences of depression, and he said to the Conservative Political Centre in 1958: 'The older ones have not forgotten. I was a Member of Parliament in those years on Tees-side. As long as I live I can never forget the impoverishment and demoralisation which all this brought with it. I am determined, as far as it lies within human power, never to allow this shadow to fall again upon our country.' That was in 1958, the same year Macmillan's reflation of the economy caused Peter Thorneycroft, Enoch Powell and Nigel Birch to resign from the Treasury.

Conservative economic policy was influenced by Keynes throughout the 1950s. The general consensus of the time about Keynesian demand management was revealed by the popular term 'Butskellism' – a merger of the names of the Conservative Chancellor R.A. Butler and the Labour leader Hugh Gaitskell. The interlude of consensus was brief, however, and the fundamental divergence in the views of the two parties reappeared in the 1960s and more vividly in the 1970s.

The major difference was that the Conservatives, while not denying the importance of a government's fiscal policy, claimed that the extent of government interference in the economy had become malignant, that excessive taxation stifled initiative and enterprise (and that Britain's low productivity figures proved it), that government control of such large parts of the economy seriously impinged on personal freedom, and that

Harold Macmillan, Prime Minister, tries for a prize at a Bromley garden fete, June 1957. Macmillan's 1959 election win was a result of the economic success of the 1950s, but he has been criticised for inflating the money supply in 1958, a move that caused Peter (now Lord) Thorneycroft, Nigel Birch and Enoch Powell to resign from the government.

the extent of monopoly power in the shape of nationalised industries was an even greater danger to individual liberty. 'A government that is big enough to give you all you want,' pointed out one contemporary Conservative, 'is big enough to take it all away.'

The idea that political freedom was inseparable from economic freedom, and that economic freedom was being endangered by government activity, gained ground in the 1970s, within the Conservative party and outside. In 1974, just before her selection as leader, Margaret Thatcher set up with Sir Keith Joseph the Centre for Policy Studies, a think-tank avowedly committed to making the case for capitalism and a free market economy. At the 1978 Conservative Conference Mrs Thatcher told the delegates, 'without free enterprise you will have neither freedom nor enterprise,' and the idea was greeted with unrestrained enthusiasm.

The clarity of Conservative thought on economics in the 1970s owed much to the work of F.A. von Hayek and Milton Friedman (winner of a Nobel prize for economics) and to the Institute of Economic Affairs who published the works of both as well as a stream of other free market economists. But it was also embedded in Conservative tradition, in the belief in diversity stemming from Edmund Burke: 'The nature of man is intricate; the objects of society are of the greatest possible complexity, and therefore no simple disposition or direction of power can be suitable either to man's nature, or to the quality of his affairs.'

CHAPTER 13
Social Life

'WE LIVE in an austere age,' said a young Conservative MP one winter afternoon in 1979. 'Disraeli would have found it very dull.'

Almost nothing underlines more sharply the transformation of the Tory party than the sea-change in its social functions from the last century to this.

When the Peels entertained (which they regularly did) in the 1830s and 1840s, in their grand town house at No. 4 Whitehall Gardens, a guest was met (according to Peel's biographer Norman Gash) by 'four or five powdered and liveried footmen in the hall who severally relieved him of his outer garments. He would then proceed upstairs with the flunkeys stationed on each landing calling out his name from one to the other until he arrived in the drawing-room to be greeted by his host. When they went in to dine, he would probably find himself eating off plate in company with thirty other guests attended by the same intimidating platoon of servants in their orange and purple livery.'

When the Peels entertained at their opulent country estate, Drayton, on the Staffordshire–Warwickshire borders, the style was more informal, but equally magnificent.

It was, of course, for Peel, as leader of the party, all part of the job. His was an age when wealth, social status and power, were inextricably intermixed; political issues were settled over the port, affairs of state decided in the lush drawing-rooms of London hostesses; the very headquarters of the party was the Carlton – a pillared and panelled gentlemen's club. The House of Lords still wielded important political power, and the country seats of the great families saw nearly as much

The grand balls and glittering dinners of the mid 19th century were an integral part of the political process, where a discreet word passed behind a pillar could settle affairs of state. The great political hostesses, Whig and Tory, ruled the social scene with iron hands, arranging marriages with the same authority that they arranged table settings.

Hughenden Manor in High Wycombe, Disraeli's country home. Political life in the 19th century revolved around the great country houses, and Disraeli adored his – even though it was bought with borrowed money and kept up by the skin of his teeth. 'When I come down to Hughenden,' he wrote, 'I pass the first week in sauntering about my park and examining all my trees, and then I saunter in the library and survey the books.'

Conviviality has been a tool in the Conservative armoury from the beginning. Smoking concerts like this one were popular features of association programmes. The party was always concerned that the social aspect might overpower the political, and agents were directed to slip in at least one political speech per concert.

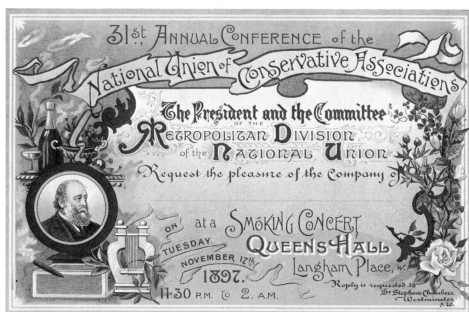

Lady Randolph Churchill (centre) with son Winston in straw boater at a garden party in Richmond, 1886. The Conservatives have always mixed social life and politics and have never been shy about exploiting their celebrities for the good of the party. The ladies flanking Jennie Churchill are wearing their Primrose League medals.

An informal gathering at Compton Place, Eastbourne, one of the residences of the Duke of Devonshire, about 1893. The Duke is far right, arm slung over chair back, with next to him Mrs Joseph Chamberlain (with white plume) and next to her the Duchess. Lady Salisbury, centre left, has her back to Lord Salisbury (seated, in top hat). Joseph Chamberlain, with his famous monocle, stands behind.

Garden party at Hatfield House, 1889. Invitations to Lord Salisbury's Jacobean house were highly prized, and one dressed accordingly. The entertainment here (lower right) was a trick-shooting cowboy.

political debate as Parliament (indeed with Parliament sitting only half the year it was as well business continued somewhere).

MPs and Peers of every party fled London as soon as Parliament rose, and then spent the recess ceaselessly trooping – from Knowsley, ancestral home of Lord Derby (which Disraeli said would be the ugliest house in England were it not for Derby's London house in St James's Square), to Hatfield, hereditary seat of the ancient intellectual Cecils; to Stowe, home of the Duke of Buckingham (who overreached himself with his entertaining and had to hastily leave the country owing £1 million); to Mentmore, the many-turreted mansion of Baron Rothschild . . . and on and round the political parade progressed. In all these stately homes the living rooms were chilly, the bedrooms icy and the draughts whistled down innumerable chimneys. But they were sumptuously furnished and lavishly staffed, and the menus were spectacular. Most of all, they were indispensable to anyone with visions of a political career.

Disraeli, a most incongruous figure amidst all this, was not to this style or manner born, neither town nor country. His own country house, Hughenden, was bought with borrowed money and kept up by the skin of his teeth. But he conquered Society just as he did Parliament and, from despised beginnings, came to be its most sought-after prize. He loved it and recorded much of it with his sharp sardonic pen. In 1835 he attended a dinner at Lord Lyndhurst's and noted it as being 'rather dull but we had a swan very white and stuffed with truffles, the best company there'. The same year he attended one of the grand masked balls given by the famous Tory hostess Lady Londonderry, at which she appeared as Cleopatra 'in a dress literally embroidered with emeralds and diamonds from top to toe.'

Above left *1890s interest in the doings
of the rich and famous was intense, and
the popular papers often carried sketches
like this 'social life at Hatfield'. Lord
Salisbury was remote ('like the Grand
Lama of Tibet,' one MP said) and
disliked frivolity; but Lady Salisbury
loved to entertain at Hatfield, and her
parties were very grand.*

Above right *Cliveden, country home of
Lord and Lady Astor on the Thames in
Buckinghamshire, which Waldorf
Astor's father gave them as a wedding
present. Nancy Astor's entertaining was
famous, partly because of her eclectic
mixing of royalty, celebrity and non-
entity. At some large parties she
persuaded her guests to wear name tags.*

Centre right *Edward VII and Queen
Alexandra at the Duchess of
Wellington's ball at Apsley House,
1908. The dazzling Edwardian
occasions where royalty, the political
establishment and the beau monde met
were avidly chronicled in the popular
press. They lent an atmosphere of fairy-
tale glamour to the essentially drab work
of government.*

Below right *Ascot, 1910: one of the
set-piece occasions of the British social
calendar, which until the First World
War automatically involved politicians.*

Arthur Balfour with Lady Londonderry at a country house party in Hertford, July 1914. She was one of the last of the great political hostesses, and this must have been one of the very last 19th-century style political house parties. War was declared on 4th August 1914.

At one of Robert Peel's dinners Disraeli arrived late to find 'some twenty-five gentlemen grubbing in solemn silence' eating (among other things) 'dried salmon, olives, caviare, wood-cock pie, foie gras, and every combination of cured herring . . .'

His own table was notoriously bad, but that did not make him any more tolerant of others; at one grand house when the champagne arrived he commented, 'Thank God for something warm.'

Disraeli adored his own country house, but he never really liked the obligatory visits to the others. His wife, Mary Ann, wrote, 'Whenever we go to a country house . . . Dizzy is not only bored, and has constant ennui, but he takes to eating as a resource; he eats at breakfast, luncheon and dinner; the result is . . . he becomes dreadfully bilious and we have to come away.'

However, he never tired of the social whirl in town – the 'glittering bustle' he called it, and at the age of 74, a widower so paper-pale that Queen Victoria feared for his health, he wrote to her explaining why he still attended so many parties: 'Lord Beaconsfield assures your Majesty that he is prudent in his social movements . . . There is a certain tact in the management of even great affairs which can only be acquired by feeling the pulse of society : . .'

Throughout the first part of the century the political 'pulse' of society did beat in the salons, which were managed with ruthless expertise by the great hostesses (to run a salon, said Disraeli, 'requires the acme of social position, knowledge & tact – great self command. If a bore comes, however inopportune, you must never by your reception of him let him suspect that he is a bore, or he will go about & tell & prevent others coming.').

Stanley Baldwin at the meet of the Old Berkshire Hunt at Chequers, the country mansion used by Prime Ministers. In its use as a venue for political meetings at the highest level Chequers parallels the country house parties of the last century, but it is held in trust for the use of Prime Ministers, not individuals, and its tenants are always temporary.

But the days of the salon, like the days of stately homes, were numbered. Both demanded not just luxurious fortunes, but also a tightly restricted power elite, preferably not more than could be accommodated at a single grand dinner. As the gradually widening franchise passed political power to more people, the salons became irrelevant, and new ways of mixing politics and sociability had to be found.

The principle that conviviality and entertainment are important political tools did not change; it was simply implemented in new ways to reach the new voters. Two organisations within the Conservative party were crucial in effecting this change: the Conservative working men's clubs and the Primrose League.

The working men's clubs began well before the formation of the National Union; indeed long before some of their members had the vote. Their usefulness to the party was urged on the National Union in 1875 by the MP for Stoke-on-Trent, who said, 'The object of converting Associations into Clubs is to enable members to obtain recreation as well as knowledge . . . We have billiard tables and every kind of amusement, together with refreshments . . . The existence of the Club . . . has had a most beneficial effect.'

The principle proved extremely sound, and 100 years later, in the 1970s, Conservative working men's clubs were still flourishing all over the country, their premises often grown far grander than the party's constituency headquarters, and their incomes grander still.

The Primrose League, although it did not set out to be, can be seen with hindsight to be an incredibly ingenious transitional device. It was another of the spontaneous movements that have arisen throughout the history of the Tory party, to the despair of its opponents: movements that appear

fortuitously, at precisely the right political moment, do their work and then quietly fade away, causing the party neither anxiety over rival power structures nor embarrassment over importunate demands.

The Primrose League, founded in 1883 originally as a memorial to Disraeli (and as a possible power base for Randolph Churchill) did two things of inestimable value for the Conservatives: it showed them how to bring the power of sociability to bear on an important section of the new electorate, and it laid the basis for the voluntary party by using women for the first time as an organised electoral force.

Leagues were organised locally by socially prominent women in the district: the wives, sisters, daughters of Tory MPs, peers, squires or clergy. Peter Marsh, who has analysed the period 1881–1902 in his book *The Discipline of Popular Government*, says, 'Into rural society, made seemingly more bleak and lonely by the bright lights of the city, the Primrose League brought colourful Mason-like ceremonial and gay festivities, whether smoking concerts or soirees or garden fetes.' 'The propaganda,' adds another writer, J.H. Robb, 'was disguised with a coating of popular entertainment, or was so surreptitiously introduced into the evening's gaiety as to be almost unnoticed.' It is noteworthy that in the election of 1885 the Conservatives did particularly well in the areas where the Primrose League was most active.

This precedent, of combining politics and entertainment, was to be followed by the party, although adapted to changing times, for the next 90 years. When women received the vote, Conservative Associations were restructured to admit them, and in so doing many of the Primrose Leagues and their activities were absorbed. The value of their pattern to a political party was vividly demonstrated again after the Second World

Sir Anthony and Lady Eden at the Conservative Agents' Ball during the Conference in Llandudno, 13th October 1956. Conservative Conferences are always more convivial than controversial, but this occasion must have called for all Eden's sang froid as it was right in the middle of the Suez crisis, and only three months before his resignation.

157

War by the tremendous growth of the Young Conservative movement. At a time when recreational activities for young people were very limited (there were not even any coffee bars), the YCs offered dances, sporting events and informal opportunities to get together under 'respectable' auspices. The movement grew huge as a result, touching an estimated quarter of a million members in the 1950s. Many leading politicians of the 1960s and 1970s began their political careers as a YC.

It was in the 1920s that the social events began to acquire their second function as fund-raisers. As pressure grew to relieve candidates and MPs of the burden of financing the association (a move codified by the Maxwell-Fyfe reforms in party organisation after the war), new sources of revenue had to be found. They were discovered in the fetes, bazaars, garden parties, annual dinners, coffee mornings, cheese-and-wines,

Harold and Lady Dorothy Macmillan. Lady Dorothy was descended from one of the great Whig families – her father was the 9th Duke of Devonshire – whose ladies so dominated the social scene of the 19th century. Modern Parliamentary wives usually remain very much in the background. The Times Guide to the House of Commons *lists every MP, his birthday, schooling and vocational background, but does not mention if he/she is married.*

Harold Macmillan, Prime Minister, solemnly does his bit at a fund-raising fete. Conservative party events have slowly changed from political intrigues (the 19th-century salons) to education-cum-propaganda exercises (Primrose League functions) to contemporary affairs where the emphasis is on fund-raising.

Only a few hours before this picture was taken (11th October 1963), Lord Home (shortly to be Sir Alec Douglas-Home) had read Macmillan's letter of resignation to an astonished party Conference. Here he dances at a Young Conservative Ball while around him the Conference seethed with speculation about the next leader.

The Lords and Commons Ski Team at Davos, 1973, for the annual competition against members of other European Parliaments. There is a sizeable, although virtually invisible, number of social activities organised among MPs and across party lines: there is a bridge team, cricket team, tennis team, football team, as well as ski team.

Edward Heath and friend set sail in Morning Cloud, 23rd May 1970. Long Parliamentary hours, shortened recesses, the inadequacy of secretarial and research assistance and the swelling volume of constituency work mean MPs have far less time than in the 19th century for extra-curricular activities. Heath was the only leader whose non-political life became as famous as his political one.

formal balls, fashion shows, treasure hunts, raffles, etc. that still fill every Conservative association's calendar. They have their counterparts at national level in the two big set-piece annual dinner dances: the Winter Ball and the Blue Ball, held in the summer.

All these activities have a two-fold purpose: they are the prime source of finance for political activities, and they are also the essential leavener and lightener of those activities. As one contemporary Conservative remarked, 'It's like Marilyn Monroe said in a film once – "You don't love a girl just because she's pretty, but it helps" – and you don't choose your political party just because the activities are entertaining . . . but it helps.'

To all the activities of the association – or as many as humanly possible – the Member of Parliament is expected to go, or send a representative in the shape of spouse or child. In a thriving association there is not a single week that does not feature at least one – usually several – events. With Parliament sitting late every weeknight, and these constituency activities every weekend, it is not surprising that the personal entertaining of Members is severely curtailed.

There is also, of course, a very different kind of Conservative Member today from the ones who elegantly dawdled in the salons of a century ago, and their style contrasts accordingly. The social revolution encouraged by the two world wars, the disappearance of servants, the increase in the numbers of working wives, the inflation of the 1960s and 1970s which cut living standards in real terms – all have had their impact on Tory MPs as on everyone else. Gone completely is the kind of opulence and affluence with which the 20th-century Lady Londonderry dazzled Ramsay Mac-donald – standing ablaze with diamonds at the top of the curving stairs in Londonderry House – or Lady Astor employed to entertain the *haut monde*

Margaret Thatcher opens the dancing at a constituency event in the early 1970s.

of Europe in the marbled halls of Cliveden. Personal entertaining by Conservative MPs in the 1970s was far more likely to be informal Sunday lunches with the hostess cooking and children and dogs tumbling underfoot, or casual suppers on nights when there was no whip.

The intense pressure at Westminster during the last half of the 1970s, when a minority Labour government kept MPs virtually chained to the division lobbies, also meant much recreation had to be found among themselves. Dining clubs proliferated, and so did recreational groups: there was a House of Commons football team, squash team, chess club, bridge club, and even language classes. Members were encouraged to take up these wholesome pursuits, and also to use the gymnasium, cycle to appointments and cut down on their calorie intake.

The results – at least among younger MPs – were visible: they were trimmer, healthier and very serious. But the Member was probably right when he said that Disraeli – who delighted in the gossip and the glamour of the salons, as well as the 'great game' of politics itself – would have found it rather dull.

CHAPTER 14

Conservatives and the Crown

THE TRANSFORMATION of the British monarchy from political power to mere (though potent) symbol is one of the great success stories of the modern age. For over a thousand years, with but a single break, an hereditary monarch has sat upon the English throne. Battles have raged, rights and perogatives have been demanded, seized and lost. Slowly the Sovereign has changed from the supreme power in the land to simply the supreme symbol. Remarkably, in the process, almost none of the trappings have been lost. Every Act of Parliament begins: 'Be it enacted by the Queen's most Excellent Majesty, by and with the advice and consent of the Lords Spiritual and Temporal, and Commons, in this present Parliament assembled . . .'

Every Parliament begins with the Sovereign in royal robes and jewel-encrusted crown reading from the resplendent throne the Queen's Speech outlining the government's ('My Government's') legislative programme.

It is all wholly symbolic, of course. The leader of the majority party in the Commons prepares the Speech; and the Royal Assent must be given to every Act that passes Parliament, even if (as Bagehot said) it provides for the execution of the Queen.

Yet the symbol, as symbol, is immeasurably powerful. The Gallup Poll estimated that 26 million people in Britain joined in the Coronation celebrations in 1953. Twenty-five years later Queen Elizabeth's Jubilee (during one of the wettest summers on record) saw such a spontaneous outpouring of affection and loyalty that even seasoned Sovereign-watchers confessed themselves amazed.

This condition – serenely settled, politically neutral, hugely popular – of the monarchy in the late 20th century has not been accomplished without strain. During the 19th century, such an outcome was by no means certain, and the monarchy owes its present shape to adroit manoeuvring both by politicians and by Sovereigns.

The Conservative party, from its earliest beginnings (which some say were in the Royalists gathered round Charles I), has always been committed to the Crown – for various reasons, and through various vicissitudes. One of the most celebrated was Robert Peel's altercation with Queen Victoria in 1839 which history calls the 'Bedchamber Crisis'. Victoria (always male dominated) was wholly under the influence of the Whig Lord Melbourne, and refused to exchange her Whiggish Ladies of the Bedchamber for Peel's suggested Tory ones. So Peel refused to form a government, although the Commons position indicated that he should. 'In respectfully submitting to your Majesty's pleasure,' he wrote to the Queen, 'and humbly returning into your Majesty's hands the important trust which your Majesty had been graciously pleased to commit to him, Sir Robert Peel trusts that your Majesty will permit him to state to your Majesty his impression with respect to the circumstances which have led to the termination of his attempt to form an Administration for the conduct of your Majesty's service . . .' He then points out the problem of the Ladies, remarks that he told her the same thing that morning, and

The 'Bedchamber Crisis' in 1839, when
Peel felt he could not form a Tory
government if the Queen still kept her
Whig ladies, showed that the monarch
was still a factor in the political struggle.

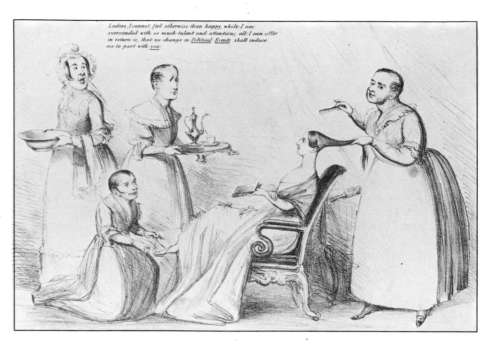

Victoria and Albert visit the great
exhibition in the Crystal Palace, 1851.
They both joined in the prevailing
attitude of confidence in commerce and
trade, and participated to the extent of
granting the imprimatur 'By
Appointment to Her Majesty . . .' to
chosen products and services.

Queen Victoria with Disraeli on a visit
to Hughenden, 1877. Suspicious of him
at first, the Queen came to hold Disraeli
in lasting affection, and when he died she
wrote: 'Never had I so kind and devoted
a Minister and very few such devoted
friends . . .' Their relationship was
unique in the annals of monarch and
Prime Minister.

concludes: 'he humbly submits to your Majesty that he is reluctantly compelled by a sense of public duty, and of the interests of your Majesty's service, to adhere to the opinion which he ventured to express to your Majesty.'

Since everyone addressed the Sovereign in these rococo terms, it was not surprising that despite her constitutional position as a 'servant of the people' Victoria did not behave like one. The Bedchamber Crisis is important, as evidence of the position of the monarch still being in a state of flux in 1839, that the political sympathies of the Ladies mattered at all.

Following this episode Victoria bore a grudge against the Tories for quite a while. In January 1840 she wrote to Prince Albert, 'The Tories really are very astonishing; . . . they do everything that they can to be personally rude to me . . . The Whigs are the only safe and loyal people . . .'

However, events, and probably Prince Albert's influence, brought about a change, and when Disraeli finally won his working majority in 1874 Victoria wrote to her eldest daughter, the Empress Frederick of Germany, that it was a wholesome sign: 'Since 46 under the gt. good & wise Sir R. Peel there has not been a Conservative Majority!! [The result of this election] shows a healthy state of the country.'

Victoria's own position was nowhere near as secure as it looks with hindsight. Disraeli was an enthusiastic supporter, but Republican movements were afoot. Frederic Harrison, writing in the *Fortnightly Review* in 1872, said, 'In London and the great cities the bulk of the working classes are republican by conviction, unless where they are perfectly indifferent. There are a score of towns in the north and centre where the republican feeling is at fever-heat . . .'

Gladstone, the Liberal Prime Minister, wrote to Earl Granville in 1870, 'the fund of credit [of Royalty] is diminishing and I do not see from whence it is to be replenished as matters now go . . .'

In fact, it was very shortly to be replenished by Disraeli creating Victoria Empress of India in 1876. Not everyone favoured this move; there was a long and exhausting struggle to get it through Parliament, but it proved in the long run to have been a master stroke, at once regilding the Crown with the exotica of Empire, and encouraging the conversion from power to symbol.

Victoria was a constitutional monarch, but she did not remain immaculately above the political ruck as do modern monarchs. She hated Gladstone and adored Disraeli, and made both views known. She had decided ideas on who should fill cabinet posts and certainly on foreign affairs. When Russia threatened Turkey she wrote to Disraeli, 'Oh, if the Queen were a man she would like to go and give those horrid Russians whose word one cannot trust such a beating!'

With relatives on or near every throne in Europe, the Queen did have a unique perspective on foreign affairs. Lord Salisbury, the Conservative Prime Minister in the 1880s and 1890s, particularly valued it. According to his daughter's biography of him, 'There was one department of knowledge in which her [Queen Victoria's] assistance was peculiarly useful to him. Drawing her facts from her large private correspondence, illuminated by old experience, she would discuss the characters and motives of the sovereigns and statesmen of Europe much in the same way that an intelligent and observant country gentleman's wife might discuss those of her country neighbours . . . It was a point of view outside the reach of official diplomats.'

The monarchy had not been popular in the earlier part of the 19th century. Victoria and, especially, Albert were viewed without enthusiasm

Disraeli made Victoria Empress of India in the spring of 1876 – a master stroke that delighted the Queen, lent increased weight to the idea of Empire and moved forward the transition of the monarch from power to symbol. In August the same year Victoria responded by making Disraeli Earl of Beaconsfield.

at first. But by the time of Victoria's Jubilees (Gold in 1887, Diamond in 1897) the Crown had been transformed into an institution of transcendent popularity. The *Times* leader for the Diamond Jubilee, 2nd June 1897, said: 'Today the eyes of the whole Empire and of millions of men beyond its pale, will be fixed upon London, and upon the great and inspiring ceremony in which we celebrate sixty years of the QUEEN's reign. They will be fixed upon the revered and beloved figure of the woman who for two full generations has represented, to so large a fraction of the human race, the principles of order, of civilization, and of rational progress. They will be fixed upon one who, in a period of all-embracing change, has offered during all these years an extraordinary instance of political and moral stability . . . Everybody feels that the QUEEN is something unique, something extraordinary, something of which all the world envies us the possession; and the multitude exults in possessing it. Length of days, width of rule beyond all precedent are hers, and she is ours.'

The Prince of Wales visits Disraeli at Hughenden, January 1880. Disraeli, then a widower, was anxious about the visit – it was mid winter, his house was small, there would be no ladies and the Prince was notoriously prone to boredom. In the end the one-night royal stay was a success. The portrait over the fireplace is Mary Ann Disraeli, on the left Queen Victoria.

Guests at a garden party, Hatfield House, 9th July 1889, in honour of the Shah of Persia (centre, with bandolier and medal). The Prince and Princess of Wales flank the Shah on the first level; Lord Salisbury is one step behind, with Lady Salisbury peeping over his shoulder. Also at this party: the Ambassadors of Spain, Russia, Germany, Turkey and France.

Victoria's Diamond Jubilee procession in Mansion House St., 1897: the growing splendour of the public spectacles disguised the waning power of the Crown. Over the last 100 years there has been a directly inverse relationship between the lavishness of royal occasions and the reality of royal power.

A shooting party at Blenheim, High Lodge, 1896, demonstrates the classic 19th-century mix of politics and royalty: standing, left to right: Earl of Gosford, Lady Emily Kingscote, Hon. Sidney Grenville, Rt Hon. G. Curzon, Gen. Ellis, Countess of Gosford, Rt Hon. A.J. Balfour, Mrs Grenfell, Sir Samuel Scott, Lord Londonderry, Lady Helen Stewart, Lady Lilian Spencer-Churchill, Mr Grenfell, HRH Prince Charles of Denmark, Viscount Curzon. Seated, left to right: Earl of Chesterfield, Lady Randolph Churchill, Duchess of Marlborough, HRH the Princess of Wales, Rt Hon. H. Chaplin, HRH Prince of Wales, Mrs George Curzon, Marchioness of Londonderry, HRH Princess Victoria, HRH Princess Charles of Denmark. On ground: Lady Sophie Scott, Duke of Marlborough, Viscountess Curzon.

Group at Sandringham includes Edward VII (far left) and the Chamberlains (second couple from the right).

King Edward VIII talks to miners in South Wales in 1936. The 20th-century convention that the monarch is non-political and non-controversial has been strictly observed, although on this occasion the King, distressed by conditions in mining villages, is reported to have startled Ministers by exclaiming, 'Something ought to be done!'

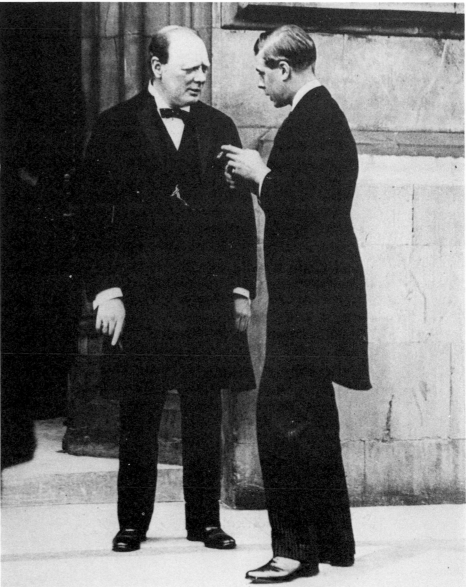

Winston Churchill and the Prince of Wales (later Edward VIII) in 1919. Churchill, like Disraeli, had an historic, almost mystic attachment to the Crown. That, as well as a long friendship, lay behind his determined defence of the King during the Abdication crisis.

This can stand as a statement of the position of the Crown: by 1897 it was secure in its symbolic role. Not least among the factors securing it were the 'great and inspiring' ceremonies that fixed 'the eyes of the whole Empire and of millions of men' upon it. As the real power of the monarchy waned, the ceremonies and rituals surrounding it became ever grander and more dazzling. Disraeli was well aware of the powers of gorgeous pageantry, and so was Lord Salisbury, during whose rule the two Jubilees took place – the second even more fabulous than the first, 'the most glittering national celebration of modern British times', according to Debrett.

After Victoria's death in 1901, the Crown was only threatened once in the next three-quarters of a century, when Edward VIII determined to marry the divorcee Wallace Simpson. Stanley Baldwin was Prime Minister at the time, and he counselled the King that such a move was incompatible with the traditions of the Crown in the 20th century. Winston Churchill, who had an attachment to the monarchy as deep and romantic as Disraeli's, felt that it was abdication that was incompatible with the traditions of the Crown. Briefly it looked as if the Conservative party would split and, much worse, as if the Crown would be dragged into controversy and its image damaged, perhaps beyond repair.

In the Bernard Partridge cartoon from Punch, *16th December 1936, Baldwin counsels the King: '. . . the throne is greater than the man.' It is a succinct statement of the Conservative attitude towards the Crown, although at the time of this crisis there was confusion over the best way to safeguard the Crown, and Churchill opposed Baldwin's approach.*

Baldwin's achievement in averting both was admired on all sides. His biographers, Middleman and Barnes, quote the papers of King Edward's private secretary: 'I am profoundly impressed by the simple skills S.B. displayed, making the outcome seem inevitable. It is like one of the great chess games – and yet only one man could have played it. If it had gone wrong, could anything have saved the monarchy?'

The Abdication crisis demonstrated vividly what the Crown had come to mean in the 20th century, and that the holder of the office was felt to have a duty, in the words of *The Times*, to be an example of 'political and moral stability'. Baldwin, and the Conservative party, believed then (and now) that the Throne tangibly represents the continuity of the British nation, visible proof that it is possible to disagree politically without rending the fabric of society. For instance, after the violent upheaval of a general election, the leaders of both parties must walk together to give homage to the Throne. The Queen's Privy Council is composed of people from both sides of the political divide, who all swear an oath to be 'a true and faithful servant unto the Queen's Majesty'. The warring sides of Parliament refer to themselves as Her Majesty's Government and Her Majesty's Loyal Opposition. Even during the most bitter inter-party strife (as during the Suez crisis) both sides remain loyal to the Crown. Governments may fall, but the Nation is secure.

The practical value of this arrangement – i.e. separating the symbol of nationhood (in which people vest their natural feelings of patriotic loyalty) from the political head (which in a democracy is necessarily partisan and temporary) – was demonstrated, according to British Conservatives, by the American trauma over removing President Nixon. In the US the ceremonial and political roles are combined in the single person of the President: it is not possible therefore to attack the political head without attacking the symbol of national unity.

Politicians from Peel to the present day have cooperated to keep the Crown a living symbol. Bagehot in 1867 is held to have made the definitive statement on the powers of a constitutional monarch: 'the sovereign has, under a constitutional monarchy such as ours, three rights – the right to be consulted, the right to encourage, the right to warn.' In order to exercise these rights the Queen is kept fully informed of all that happens in 'her' government. Red boxes of state papers and correspond-

VE Day at Buckingham Palace:
Princess Elizabeth, Queen Elizabeth
(now the Queen Mother), Churchill,
King George VI, Princess Margaret.

The Prime Minister and Mrs Churchill
leave Buckingham Palace for
Westminster Abbey and the Coronation
of Queen Elizabeth II in 1952.
Politicians come and go, but the
substance of the Coronation ceremony
has remained much the same for over a
thousand years.

The Queen (18th October 1963) leaves King Edward VII hospital after seeing Macmillan. He had sent her his letter of resignation, and she was about to ask Alec Douglas-Home to be Prime Minister. It was one of the few occasions this century when the monarch played a visible part in the political drama. With the Queen is her Private Secretary Sir Michael Adeane.

The annual State Opening of Parliament: the Queen arrives in the royal coach at the entrance of the House of Lords in part of a ritual that has existed for centuries.

Edward Heath, Prime Minister, between royal ladies (Princess Alexandra and Princess Anne) at the Court v. King match at Wimbledon, 1970. Wimbledon, like Ascot, is a fixture of the British social calendar, one of the few places left where royalty, the political world and the beau monde meet on neutral ground.

ence arrive continuously at the palaces, the Royal Yacht or wherever the Queen happens to be. Every evening when Parliament is sitting the Vice Chamberlain (one of the majority party Whips) writes a 'telegram' of what has happened that day, which is whisked to the Palace at 6 o'clock so the Queen can read it while dressing for dinner. It is a personal report, dating from the time when the task was the Prime Minister's. 'You write whatever you think is important,' said a former Conservative Vice Chamberlain, 'sometimes what happens in the tea room is more important than what happens in the Chamber.'

Perhaps the most important part of the Monarch's 'political' role is the appointment of the Prime Minister. Now that both parties hold formal elections for their leaders this choice is practically limited – although not constitutionally dictated. But before the Conservatives set up their voting procedure in 1964, there were at least three instances this century when the Tory leadership was unclear and the Monarch appeared to have a choice: in 1922, with Bonar Law desperately ill, the party's choice was uncertain between Lord Curzon and Stanley Baldwin. The King came down for Baldwin, a decision with far reaching consequences. In 1957, when Anthony Eden resigned, it was very moot whether R. A. Butler or Macmillan would be called to form the government. And in 1963, when Macmillan resigned, the choice was even wider. The 'sense' of the party was communicated to the Sovereign in each case, but constitutionally he (she) could consult anyone to help determine the choice.

Political participation, however, is not the point of the monarchy for Conservatives. Its major significance for the Tories was defined by Disraeli over 100 years ago, and (as with so much of Disraeli) is startlingly relevant today: 'Gentlemen, the influence of the Crown is not confined merely to political affairs. England is a domestic country. Here the home is revered and the hearth is sacred. The nation is represented by a family – the Royal Family; and if that family is educated with a sense of responsibility and sentiment of public duty, it is difficult to exaggerate the salutary influence they may exercise over a nation. It is not merely an influence upon manners; it is not merely that they are a model for refinement and for good taste – they affect the heart as well as the intelligence of the people; and in the hour of public adversity, or in the anxious conjuncture of public affairs, the nation rallies round the Family and the Throne, and its spirit is animated and sustained by the expression of public affection.'

Index

Acknowledgements

A popular history necessarily owes an enormous debt to serious scholars, and I would like to acknowledge with gratitude and admiration by particular debt to the following works. Robert Blake: *The Conservative Party from Peel to Churchill*; *Disraeli*; *Andrew Bonar Law, The Unknown Prime Minister*. Norman Gash: *Sir Robert Peel*; *Politics in the Age of Peel*. Robert McKenzie: *British Political Parties*; *Angels in Marble*. H.J. Hanham: *Elections and Party Management, Politics in the Time of Disraeli and Gladstone*; *The Nineteenth Century Constitution*. Robert Rhodes James: *The British Revolution* (2 volumes); *Churchill, A Study in Failure 1900–1939*; *Ambitions and Realities, British Politics 1964–70*. Keith Middlemas and John Barnes: *Baldwin*. Peter Marsh: *The Discipline of Popular Government: Lord Salisbury's Domestic Statecraft*. John Ramsden: *The Age of Balfour and Baldwin*. David Clarke: *The Conservative Party*. Ian Gilmour: *Inside Right, A Study of Conservatism*. Lord Butler: *The Conservatives, A History from their Origins to 1965; The Art of the Possible*. David Butler and Anne Sloman: *British Political Facts 1900–1975*. The memoirs of Sir Winston Churchill, Harold Macmillan and Lord Home have been invaluable, as have the excellent Nuffield Election Studies from 1945.

I would also like to acknowledge with many thanks the help given me by Geoffrey Block of the Conservative Party Archives, the photo library at Conservative Central Office, the library at the House of Commons, and the many contemporary Conservative MPs who have generously given me the benefit of their experience and advice. Particular thanks are due to Andrew Rowe who was the first to say, 'What the Party needs is an illustrated history!'

Last and most important, I would like to record my gratitude and admiration to John Moore: MP, critical editor, husband and friend.

Photographic Acknowledgements

The illustrations on the following pages are Crown Copyright, reproduced with the permission of the Controller of Her Majesty's Stationery Office 125 bottom, 126 top, 126 bottom.
The cartoon on page 169 is reproduced by permission of *Punch*, the Low cartoon on page 135 right by permission of the *Evening Standard*.

COLOUR
Author 54 bottom; John Bethell, St Albans 25 bottom, 53 top, 53 bottom right, 100; Camera Press, London – Lionel Cherruault 143 top; Central Press Photos, London 72 top; Hamlyn Group Picture Library/Country Life Books – John Webb 53 bottom left; 98–99; Keystone Press Agency, London 125 top, 143 centre, 143 bottom; Malcolm Lewis, London 97; Mansell Collection, London 26–27, 54 top; National Portrait Gallery, London 25 top; Popperfoto, London 71 top, 71 bottom, 72 bottom; Press Association, London 144; The Marquess of Salisbury, Hatfield House 28 top, 28 bottom.

BLACK AND WHITE
Associated Newspapers, London 115 bottom; Associated Press, London 68 bottom right; Bassano & Vandyk, London 22, 23 top; BIPPA, London 92; BBC Hulton Picture Library, London 16 bottom, 30 top, 36 top right, 49 top, 68 left, 88 top, 90, 96 top, 101 bottom, 104 top, 104 bottom, 110 bottom right, 111, 112 centre, 113 bottom, 119, 120 bottom, 127 left, 129 left, 132 bottom, 134 top left, 134 centre, 139, 145, 146 right, 147, 155, 156, 164 bottom, 166 top, 167 top, 167 bottom; Camera Press, London 34 bottom, 146 left; Central Press, London 19 bottom, 29 top, 29 bottom, 31 top, 33, 74 top, 106 top, 115 top, 154 top right, 159 bottom, 171 top, 171 bottom; Century Newspapers, Belfast 130; Winston Churchill 129 right; Conservative Party Archives, London 18 top, 38 top left, 44, 46, 52 bottom, 70 top, 76 bottom, 77, 78 left, 78 right, 79 top, 79 bottom, 80 top, 80 bottom, 108, 109 top, 117, 133 left, 138, 161, 166 bottom; Conservative Working Men's Club, Croydon 132 top right; Crown Copyright, Central Office of Information, London 45, 106 bottom; *Daily Telegraph*, London 58; Jack Esten, *Illustrated* 50 top; Fox Photos, London 170 top; Gernsheim Collection, Humanities Research Center, University of Texas at Austin 110 top; Douglas Glass 30 bottom; International News Photo 55; Keystone Press Agency, London 23 bottom, 24, 31 bottom, 32, 34 top, 41 right, 43, 50 bottom, 56, 57 top, 57 bottom, 73, 81 top, 81 bottom, 84, 93, 105, 107, 116 top, 116 bottom, 118 top, 118 bottom, 128 bottom, 136, 137 left, 137 right, 148 top, 148 bottom, 149, 150, 158, 159 top, 160 bottom; Mansell Collection, London 20 top, 20 bottom, 35, 36 left, 36 bottom right, 37, 60, 61, 62, 66 top, 66 centre, 67, 86 top, 86 bottom, 87 top, 87 bottom, 88 bottom, 89, 95 top, 95 bottom, 96 centre, 96 bottom, 101 top, 109 bottom, 110 bottom left, 112 top, 112 bottom, 113 top, 120 centre, 121 top, 121 bottom, 123 bottom, 124 top, 124 bottom, 131, 132 top left, 134 top right, 140 left, 140 top right, 140 bottom right, 141 top, 141 centre, 141 bottom, 142 top, 142 bottom, 151, 152 top, 152 centre, 152 bottom, 154 centre, 154 bottom, 164 top, 164 centre, 165; Mirror Group Newspapers/Syndication International 114 right, 122 left, 128 top; *Morning Star*, London 91 bottom; National Portrait Gallery, London 14 top, 14 bottom, 15 left, 16 top, 63, 64; Pictorial Press, London 51; P.N.A. 41 left; Planet News, London 70 bottom, 157; Popperfoto, London 17 top, 17 bottom, 19 top, 38 top right, 38 bottom, 40 top, 49 bottom, 50 centre, 68 top right, 69, 82, 94, 102 bottom, 123 top, 127 right, 133 right, 134 bottom, 168 top, 168 bottom; Poy, *Daily Mail*, London 91 bottom; Press Association, London 21 bottom, 42, 75, 76 top; The Marquess of Salisbury, Hatfield House 15 right, 47 top, 47 bottom, 48 top, 48 bottom, 64 bottom, 153 top, 153 bottom, 154 top left; Sport & General Press Agency, London 21 top, 52 top, 83 top, 83 bottom; Syndication International, London 122 right; D.C. Thomson 162; *The Times*, London 172; John Topham Picture Library, Edenbridge 40 bottom; Topical Press Agency, London 39, 170 bottom; Stanley White 74 bottom; Reece Winstone, Bristol 103.